Praise for *One and Only*

"[Sandler] delves deeply, thoughtfully, and humorously into history, culture, politics, religion, race, economics, and of course, scientific research. . . . Will she or won't she have another? The beauty of her in-depth c̶ ons she poses make this one seen

—Lori G Review

"There is a welcome strain of argument undergirding this well-researched and lively book: looking out for your own happiness is not inconsistent with being a good mother. This is a vital part of the conversation that's not being discussed in the chatter surrounding middle-class parenting."

—Jessica Grose, *The New Republic*

"Sandler makes her case with zeal. . . . [She] certainly has a dramatic touch with language, and in her book she adduces a prodigious amount of reporting, data and research. . . . The data Sandler cite speak convincingly to the proposition that only children, at the very least, should not be negatively stereotyped."

—*The Washington Post*

"[A] thoughtful, well-reasoned book. . . . Sandler writes movingly."

—*The Boston Globe*

"[Sandler] blends a wealth of research with personal anecdote to argue that only children in fact grow up with significant advantages."

—*The Week*

"The impressive depth of Sandler's reporting . . . lends necessary rigor to important, emotionally complex questions of family size, parental well-being, and public policy. The result is a swift and absorbing read. . . . Her fervently argued book may be enough to change your mind and the national conversation."

—*Psychology Today*

"[Sandler] cuts at the core of one of modern women's most stubborn, self-defeating beliefs—that unless we are everything to all people, we are nothing, that our worth is tied up in our limitless capacity (at least when it comes to caring for others), that we don't actually deserve to live a selective life and take or leave a number of energy-sucking pursuits."

—Courtney Martin, CNN

"I couldn't put it down. The book—despite what the cover says—isn't really about only children. This is what it is: It's about relationships with our kids, our spouse, our parents, and most importantly with ourselves. It's also about how scientific studies are often publicized to suit our own notions of right and wrong. Or ignored, if they don't match our morals. . . . Lauren isn't proselytizing; she's just stating it like it is. Seductively honest."

—Randi Hutter Epstein, *The Huffington Post*

"[Sandler's] questions have never been more relevant. . . . *One and Only* is peppered with lyrical anecdotes of her daily life (a tangle of limbs in a 'family hug,' a bedtime standoff) that seem to remind us of every family's own intense, wonderful, maddening dynamic."

—Nona Willis Aronowitz, *The American Prospect*

"Journalist Lauren Sandler argues persuasively that being born a singleton isn't a tragedy, but a gift—both for a kid and their parents."

—Sarah Weir, *Yahoo*

"Why, Sandler asks, are prejudices about 'selfish' and 'maladjusted' single kids (and their parents) so widespread in our culture, despite much evidence to the contrary? Part of the answer has to do with myths about the happiness of singletons and their families, which Sandler debunks, but the book has a broader scope that makes it worthwhile for anyone interested in government policy and contemporary American culture."

—Katherine Stewart, *Religion Dispatches*

"*One and Only* should be required reading for any parent who wants to have only one child but thinks they should have two 'for the sake of the children.' It should also be read by parents of multiples who feel that their one-child peers are somehow 'less' as parents."

—Michelle Richmond, *San Francisco Journal of Books*

"*One and Only* has been a great solace to mothers of only children (this writer included)."

—Wendy Paris, *The Jewish Week*

"Sandler delivers a work of fierce reporting, tender storytelling, and clear-eyed cultural analysis."

—Susan Cain, author of *Quiet*

"Lauren Sandler's book is eloquent, articulate, persuasive, and whip-smart. But its greatest virtue may be its restraint. This is, thank goodness, no faddish argument for only children. *One and Only* is something much wiser and much, much more important. It's a plea to disregard our facile (and demonstrably incorrect) stereotypes about family size and accept a universal truth: *one size does not fit all.*"

—Daniel Smith, *New York Times*
bestselling author of *Monkey Mind*

"Sandler's thought-provoking—and often surprising—analysis will fascinate anyone interested in how family circumstances shape our lives."

—Gretchen Rubin, *New York Times*
bestselling author of *The Happiness Project*

"Sandler powerfully debunks generations of myths about the loneliness, selfishness, and general neuroticism of only children. Her book is a must-read both for adult only children and parents of 'just' one—and an eye-opener for anyone interested in a fresh look at the meaning of connectedness."

—Judith Warner, *New York Times*
bestselling author of *Perfect Madness*

"Sandler weaves a gripping tale of motherhood and modernity, bypassing the mommy wars to expose the wider conditions in which parenting choices are made. She's one of the most cogent commentators on feminism and family there is."

—Deborah Siegel, PhD, coeditor of *Only Child*

"This book, like everything Lauren Sandler writes, is lush and riveting. Only children or people who have only children will find comfort in these pages, and parents generally should read it to understand their own choices."

—Alissa Quart, author of *Hothouse Kids*

"With wit, warmth, and keen intelligence, Sandler skewers the myths about only children and their parents. If you're tired of all the foolish generalizations, buy several copies of this book and hand them out at the playground!"

—Liza Featherstone, author of *Selling Women Short*

"Onlies, parents of onlies, and readers still on the fence will find the book illuminating and affirming."

—*Publishers Weekly*

"[T]he author's argument dispels stereotypes of 'onlies' and raises provocative questions about the American tendency toward prioritizing and even elevating parenthood over relationships, individuality, social networks and other aspects of adulthood, sometimes to the detriment of the family. Recommended as an alternative perspective on an often emotionally fraught discussion."

—*Kirkus Reviews*

ALSO BY LAUREN SANDLER

Righteous: Dispatches from the Evangelical Youth Movement

ONE AND ONLY

The Freedom of
Having an Only Child,
and the Joy of Being One

LAUREN SANDLER

Simon & Schuster Paperbacks

New York London Toronto Sydney New Delhi

FOR JUSTIN AND DAHLIA

Simon & Schuster Paperbacks
A Division of Simon and Schuster, Inc.
1230 Avenue of the Americas
New York, NY 10020

Copyright © 2013 by Lauren Sandler

All rights reserved, including the right to reproduce this book or portions thereof in any form whatsoever. For information address Simon & Schuster Paperbacks Subsidiary Rights Department, 1230 Avenue of the Americas, New York, NY 10020.

First Simon & Schuster paperback edition June 2014

SIMON & SCHUSTER PAPERBACKS and colophon are registered trademarks of Simon & Schuster, Inc.

For information about special discounts for bulk purchases, please contact Simon & Schuster Special Sales at 1-866-506-1949 or business@simonandschuster.com.

The Simon & Schuster Speakers Bureau can bring authors to your live event. For more information or to book an event, contact the Simon & Schuster Speakers Bureau at 1-866-248-3049 or visit our website at www.simonspeakers.com.

Designed by Nancy Singer

Manufactured in the United States of America

10 9 8 7 6 5 4 3 2 1

The Library of Congress has cataloged the hardcover edition as follows:
Sandler, Lauren.
One and only: the freedom of having an only child, and the joy of being one / Lauren Sandler.
pages cm
Includes bibliographical references.
1. Only child. 2. Family size. 3. Families. I. Title.
HQ777.3.S26 2013
306.874—dc23
                                                        2013000707
ISBN 978-1-4516-2695-7
ISBN 978-1-4516-2696-4 (pbk)
ISBN 978-1-4516-2697-1(ebook)

CONTENTS

CONTENTS

INTRODUCTION

IT'S NOT WHAT YOU THINK

This is not a memoir, but to conform to what's expected of an only child, let me start with myself.

My mother was deeply devoted to raising me. To have a happy kid, she figured she needed to be a happy mother, and to be a happy mother, she needed to be a happy person. To do that, she had to preserve her authentic self, which she could not imagine doing with a second child.

"It was all about me," she freely admits to me one night, in a way that simultaneously makes my chest swell with pride (feminism!) and my shoulders contract with a cringe (selfishness!). My parents are in Brooklyn for a weekend visit. It's getting close to midnight, and my mother and I are in our nightgowns, tucked under the covers of the sleep couch. My husband, Justin, and my dad are nursing their beers, feet propped up on the foot of the bed.

"When you were three," she goes on, "I thought I was pregnant. I stayed up all night making a pros and cons list. By morning, it was clear to me I couldn't have another kid." She easily recites the "con" litany: she could continue her career uninterrupted, stay in the apartment she loved instead of trading urbanity for a suburban existence, maintain a certain level of independence, and worry less about money.

I interrupt her to ask about the "pro" list. I have no idea what she's going to say. She's never so much as suggested that there would be a competing list. Instead of replying, she continues, "I just would have had to be a totally different person with another kid. My life would have utterly changed. Luckily, it turned out I wasn't pregnant."

"I get that, Mom. I do. But what about the other list?" She's silent. My father studies the label on his beer bottle. "Dad, what did you want?" I ask.

My father looks up at me. "I so loved parenting; I always wanted the experience to be varied, to go on," he says quietly. A vocal strain belies his next words: "But you know me. I'm not a regretful person." He looks back down at his bottle. "What can I say," he says. "The years passed. It became the choice. Here we are." He grins at me. "Where we are isn't half bad, I might add. It just took me some time to get used to the idea."

It takes us all some time to get used to the idea. As only children, we have to get used to lacking something that the majority of people have for better or for worse. As parents who choose to stop at one, we have to get used to the nagging feeling that we are choosing for our own children something they can never undo. We're deciding not to know two kids splashing in the bubble bath, playing in the pile of raked leaves, whispering under the cover of darkness, teasing each other at the dinner table, holding hands at our funerals.

Everyone seems to think they know who we are, both singletons and parents of singletons. We are the selfish ones. I must be doubly so, as an only child myself, and the mother of one. Who else but an only child would have the sense of self-importance to write about being one, much less suggest that other people consider it for themselves? But after investigating the whole matter, let me offer this spoiler: I don't buy it.

Lonely. Selfish. Maladjusted. These are the words that Toni Falbo, the leading researcher in the small field of only child studies, uses to explain our image of only children. Falbo lists these characteristics so often, they tend to run together as a single word: *lonelyselfishmaladjusted.*

Why did this idea take hold? The academic basis of the miserable singleton specimen was the work of one man, who famously lectured, "Being an only child is a disease in itself." Granville Stanley Hall was a leader of the late-nineteenth-century child-study movement and had a national network of study groups called Hall Clubs that spread his teachings. Not a bad way to disseminate his 1896 study, "Of Peculiar and Exceptional Children," which described only children as permanent misfits. Never mind that Hall also openly fetishized his own agrarian, big-brood upbringing and disdained the smaller-family urbanity that was creeping into a rapidly industrializing country. Just consider that Hall—and every other fledgling psychologist—knew close to nothing about credible research practices.

Yet for decades, academics and advice columnists alike spread his conclusion that an only child could not develop the same capacity for adjustment as children with siblings. "Overprivileged, asocial, royally autonomous . . . self-centered, aloof and overly intellectual," is the culturally perceived "unchallengeable given" of the only child, as sociologist Judith Blake wrote in her 1989 book *Family Size and Achievement,* which attempted to scientifically dismantle aspects of the stereotype. Later generations of scholars tried to correct the record, but their findings never filtered into popular parenting discourse. The "peculiar" only child had permeated pop culture, from oddball sidekicks in eighties sitcoms to demon children in horror films. Hellion only children are legendary on screen: *The Shining, The Exorcist, Friday the Thirteenth,* and *The Butcher Boy* are all films that rely on a seriously psychotic singleton (yes, even *Psycho*) to terrorize their innocent costars.

It's not just fright-fests that traffic in typecasting only children. Name a genre, and there's a list of characters to give the stereotype narrative heft and form: Tom Ripley, Veruca Salt, Eric Cartman. Even superheroes fit the stereotype, misfit loners incapable of truly connecting with citizens of the real world, suspicious in their overintelligence, often fighting against their privilege. Batman, Superman, Spider-Man, Iron Man—only children all. But this troubled image projected onto the popular consciousness can be complicated by the real-life heroism of some singletons whose ability to connect with others was central to their own superpowers: you might not know it, but Mahatma Gandhi was an only child too.

Around the time my mother stayed awake on the couch with her pros and cons list, she met with the administrators of my nursery school to convince them to extend hours until six o'clock in the evening, to accommodate the needs of working parents. The next morning a squadron of mothers cornered her at the door to the school. Wearing pajamas under their trench coats, they allowed her to drop me off before moving in for the attack. "We've been waiting for you," they said. They were fundamentally opposed to her suggestion of an extended day. "We wanted to tell you our children are our only priority."

During an interview with British psychologist Bernice Sorensen, who wrote a book called *The Only-Child Experience & Adulthood,* I mention that my mother chose to stop at one and I am considering the same for my family. Her response is to snap, "So, your mother is a narcissist, and you're one too if you make that choice, and you will probably ensure the same future for your daughter. Isn't that what you're telling me?" Let's just say she's one singleton who didn't enjoy the experience.

The majority of parents say they have second children for the sake of their first child, or at least that's what they've told Gallup pollsters for decades. But it's hard to imagine anything that can be reduced to a simple survey question, much less an issue that layers notions of family, happiness, responsibility, legacy—life and death itself, when you think about it. Still, we all know that there's truth in this response: first children tend to be a choice parents make to fulfill their own lives and a second child tends to be a choice parents make to fulfill the life of their existing child.

Some people believe that a family with one child isn't really a family, although I defy anyone to strictly define familial normalcy today. Kids are increasingly—and happily—raised by same-sex parents (in fact, recent studies suggest that lesbian mothers are the best parents of all). Divorce is as common as not. In vitro fertilization has pushed the possible age of conception into the midforties. Siblings are almost as likely stepbrothers and stepsisters as they are the children of their own biological parents.

Such developments in the way we define a family produce questions about how to define an only child. Statisticians tend to use the rule that if you spent your first seven years raised as the sole child in a household, you count as one. But I've met plenty of people who consider themselves onlies because they felt estranged from stepsiblings, and others who would never think of themselves as singletons, despite an age gap of a dozen-odd years, because of how close they are to a brother or sister. These definitions are murky at best. Some only-child experiences and tendencies will apply to some situations (e.g., the seven-year rule works well when understanding selfishness or achievement), and not to others (e.g., even if your sister was in college when you were born, confronting the death of a parent would be radically different without her). It's erroneous to think there is such a thing as "normal"—much less that we should aspire to such a concept.

And still, one of America's most successful exports has been the cultural assertion that joyful families are big families: from *Meet Me in St. Louis* to the *Cheaper by the Dozen* remakes, the Partridges to the Duggars. One young woman in China, who was raised in a rural village populated by a generation of only children, tells me she never knew what a "normal" family looked like until the Chinese television authority permitted reruns of *Growing Pains* when she was in middle school. "The Seaver family was the first 'real family' I had ever seen," she says, admitting a crush on Kirk Cameron and excitedly telling me that the actor who played Ben Seaver married a gal from Shanghai. "They seemed so happy together—why wouldn't I want that?"

"Nobody wants that—that's not what people imagine for their lives," says sociologist Philip Morgan at the Carolina Population Center when I ask him to discuss the rising number of only children. In surveys that ask young women how many children they'd like to have, ultimately and ideally, no one says they'd choose to stop at one child, he tells me. To me, that's like asking a tween girl what her perfect wedding looks like. My childhood fantasy was to get married on an island in Boston's Public Garden in a dress my grandmother would take me shopping for in Paris, with a swing band and guests encircling me and my groom in floating Swan Boats. Instead, my grandmother was confined to a nursing ward, I wore a two-hundred-dollar off-the-rack dress, we got hitched at my parents' house and danced to a six-hour mix we made that blew out my dad's speakers. My grandmother's absence aside, it was grand. We envision one thing; we live with another. Our ideals change in concert with our emerging realities—even more so if, as we develop, we opt to interrogate what we thought we wanted, and why we thought we wanted it.

Here are some things I want: I want to do meaningful work. I want to travel. I want to eat in restaurants and drink in bars. I want to go to movies and concerts. I want to read novels. I want to marinate in solitude. I want to have friendships that regularly sustain and exhilarate me. I want a romantic relationship that involves daily communication beyond interrogatives and imperatives—I want to be *known*. And I want to snuggle with my daughter for as long as she'll let me, being as present in her life as I can while giving her all the space she needs to discover life on her own terms. I want full participation: in the world, in my family, in my friendships, and in my own actualization.

In other words, to have a happy kid, I figure I need to be a happy mother, and to be a happy mother, I need to be a happy person. Like my mother, I feel that I need to make choices within the limits of reality—which means considering work, finances, pleasure—and at the moment I can't imagine how I could possibly do that with another kid. Someone once asked Alice Walker if women (well, woman artists) should have children. She replied, "They should have children—assuming this is of interest to them—but only one." Why? "Because with one you can move," she said. "With more than one, you're a sitting duck."

Still, I agonize every time I see my daughter doting on a friend's baby, just as my own heart has a tendency to devour itself whole when I take a new tiny person in my arms, inhaling its sweetness, nuzzling that soft neck, thrilling to every smile and coo. When my daughter was born, after all my anxiety about how I'd never changed a diaper, all my avowing that I prefer living things who can verbally communicate, all my certainty that bonding would be an infinite process, and all my fear that I would never again live life on my own terms—well, I held my girl, just moments old, and I simply knew what to do. My confidence and capability stunned me. Justin's too—though I always knew he was up to the task. And yet when I try to imagine doing it again, I feel even greater doubt than I did the first time.

There are plenty of parents who deeply want more than one child and are willing to make profound compromises to have the family they want. These are not people beset with ambivalence or fear that they will forever damage their first child by not offering it the gift of a sibling. These are parents who know what they're in for and know what sacrifices they're willing to make for it. The last thing we need is another person telling women what they should or should not do with their fallopian tubes, their finances, and their futures. I'm not here to preach the Gospel of the Only Child.

What I'm saying is this: when we obsess about which stroller to buy, or whether to go with cloth or paper diapers, or whether organic produce is a must, or whether Mozart or Mingus will make our babies brilliant, or if we've overscheduled or underscheduled or overfed or underfed or overvaccinated or undervaccinated our kids, yet we fail to consider whether we should actually be *having* another child, it's time to change the conversation.

We ask when people are having *kids*—never *a kid*, never one child at a time, which is how it usually happens. If a kid has no siblings, it's assumed that there's a hush-hush reason for it: that parents don't like parenthood (because they are selfish), or they care about their status—work, money, materialism—more than their kid (because they are selfish), or they waited too long (because they are selfish).

Over the past century, adulthood has come to promise more than just duty, but pleasure. We search for a partner who will satisfy our desires, develop a career that reflects our strengths, build a life that suits not just our needs, but our wants. Despite the fact that it's no longer possible to have a middle-class life on one income—and often not even on two—we envision a liberated existence, one of satisfaction and fulfillment, a life built upon intentionality and individualism rather than obligation and role filling. This liberated adulthood exists at odds with parenting.

It doesn't take forced population control to raise the number of a country's only children—the relative incompatibility of motherhood and modernity has taken care of that. Germany, Austria, Spain, Italy, Japan, and Korea all have fertility rates of less than 1.4 per woman, about half the number of kids women in those countries were having in the seventies. While family policy that helps to manage the collision between work and parenthood—and particularly motherhood—is nearly nonexistent in the United States, governments elsewhere have recently inserted themselves into the business of families. This is mainly to address the fact that so many people have decided the cost of children isn't worth it.

In the early sixties, Europe represented almost thirteen percent of the world's population. About a century later, those numbers are projected to drop to about five percent. Women have consciously refused parenthood in favor of education, careers, and a greater degree of freedom, or have delayed their fertility until biology made the choice for them. In this depopulation "crisis," as the European Union has defined it, public support has become indispensable to make the sacrifices required of parents more manageable, and thus more palatable. In the more secular regions of the United States, our fertility looks like Europe's, but you'd never know by looking at our national averages.

That's because so many Americans commit to a family-values ethic that lionizes maternal sacrifice and exalts large households. Back when the mandate "to be fruitful and multiply" was first intoned, it had a purpose. The more you bred, the more likely your family line would survive—crucial wisdom in the days of high infant and child mortality. A biological imperative became a religious one, imposed by spiritual leaders and faith communities. If you comb the World Value Survey, you'll find religiosity and family size go hand in hand. Because of the very relationship between faith and fertility, a wide stripe of thinkers, be they demographers, anthropologists, or evolutionary psychologists, believe the religious will inherit the earth. They believe parents like myself who deeply value an extra-familial identity will simply be outbred over time by the fruitfully conservative.

In the United States, the recession has dramatically reshaped people's childbearing intentions. This happens during all financial meltdowns: the Great Depression saw single-child families spike at nearly thirty percent of all families, and that was back when onlies were still considered an anomaly. But today it seems more extreme than ever because of the price individuals pay to attain a place in our shrinking middle class. A Guttmacher Institute survey recently found that two-thirds of Americans feel they can't afford to have a baby in the current economy. No wonder: our total student loan debt alone—of $1 trillion—is forcing people to delay having their first child or preventing them from considering a second one. Some demographers estimate that nationwide single-child families might surge to Manhattan rates of more than thirty percent. But that doesn't mean anyone feels good about it.

As desires and identities evolve, we continue to deify old myths instead of creating new ones. We delay childbirth in our classrooms and boardrooms, working and wishing, dating and dishing. Our bodies get older. Our lives get crazier. Our dreams expand instead of contract. By the time we're ready to admit that we'll never be ready, it's tougher to conceive. And even if it's not, it's tough to conceive of doing it again. This is the story of most people in the developed world: we're in a fertility panic. But there's a different, if related, panic that governments and grandparents alike ignore. It's the terror of raising an only child.

We all know that stereotypes must be based on some reality, even if they reflect a warped and expanded version of the truth. But in considering the components of a *lonelyselfishmaladjusted* identity, only children are not who you'd expect. I'll unpack the myth at length, but here's a teaser. On loneliness: as kids, we're usually fine. As adolescents, we're often disempowered and isolated. As adults, we face the logistical and existential nightmare of our parents' aging and death alone. But the good news is we develop the strongest primary relationships with *ourselves*. On selfishness: as long as we go to school, we're plenty socialized to play well with others. On maladjustment: we're fine. Overall, we're pretty fantastic.

What the stereotype largely ignores are two areas where we tend to separate from the pack. The first is achievement. Simply, we tend to succeed at significantly higher rates than people raised with siblings, whether it's at school or in our professional endeavors. Solitary pursuits like reading train our focus and curiosity, and the verbally rich environment of life among adults accelerates our learning. Secondly, everything in a family without siblings is amplified. That means that the dynamics of our parents' marriages—and divorces—and the way boundaries and needs are policed and expressed in our familial equations tend to have an augmented effect on us. Siblings provide diversity and distraction in a family. We have none of that. Instead, we have at times a ferocious intensity—for good and for bad. I found this common intensity conspicuously absent in the data, but unequivocally present in lived experience, threaded through my interviews, my biographical reading, and my own family. As one psychologist murmured quietly to me, "It's a very powerful way to grow up."

By demystifying the perceived problem of the only child, I want to legitimize a conversation about the larger societal costs of having more than one. It's not just a question of who wins the culture wars, but also who pays for them. *Who will support our elderly? Who will be our labor force?* But there's not just the economy to consider, there's the environment. Isn't it better for the planet to have fewer megaconsuming SUV drivers and airplane passengers addicted to air conditioning and cheeseburgers?

Yet nobody has more babies to boost the economy, nor do most people stop at one to save the planet. No other decision is as personal. And yet so many of us are beholden to social and cultural pressure, to the threat of stereotypes. If parents no longer felt they had to have second children to keep from royally screwing up their first, would the majority of them still do it? What if those of us who don't otherwise feel compelled to have more kids opted instead for greater autonomy and self-fulfillment? If the literature tells us—in hundreds of studies, over decades of research—that my kid isn't better off with a sibling, and it's not something I can truly say I want for myself, then who is this choice serving?

When our internal desires clash with accepted wisdom, it's incumbent upon us to wonder why. I believe that when we interrogate our assumptions, we find they're usually coming from the culture, which needs us to behave. We need to be more assertive in questioning why exactly we believe our children need siblings. Because if I'm going to choose to have another one, while billions of other people do the same, I should be able to know the reason.

And if it's not because I want to—I mean, really *want* to—have another child, there's a body of supposed knowledge I need to start questioning. For myself. For my daughter. And for the world I brought her into. Instead of making a choice to enlarge our families based on stereotypes or cultural pressure, we can instead make that most profound choice our most purely independent one. It might even feel like something people rarely associate with parenting: it might feel like freedom.

ONE

THE UNTEACHABLE EAGLE

n the beginning, there was land. Land that needed to be planted and tended, animals that needed to be minded and slaughtered. A family was a workforce. The more children a family had—once they were of able working age, by ten years old—the more people could help turn surviving into thriving. Children were life insurance. Infant mortality was high; life expectancies were short—just two centuries ago only half of all children survived past age five—and blood meant everything. The lesson was clear: parent or perish. A labor unit of one was a close second to nothing. Furthermore, throughout the centuries when one's culture essentially began and ended at home, the society of a lone child was a hearth of darkness.

Of course, I didn't dust my hands off on a pinafore apron before I sat down to write this—modernity gradually emerged. Children maintained their usefulness, continuing to pitch in with some light farming or manufacturing, minding the shop or the little ones, and entertaining one another. But big families were no longer a necessity for a family's survival. And yet the perceived darkness of the single-child family loomed. Only children posed no threat to a family's survival, but they were objects of scorn all the same. They were a mealy, sour, mysterious fruit. And their parents were to be pitied, or judged, or both.

Folk advice and popular myth remained the source of expertise as far as family dynamics and child development were concerned; we had not yet witnessed the birth of psychology. Once theories of the mind, and how it is shaped by environment, began to emerge with some legitimacy, they did so without what could be considered scientific testing. But, fittingly, they left the enigmatic and suspicious singleton just how he was perceived—alone.

Until Granville Stanley Hall, whose popularity and influence was monumental. Sigmund Freud made his first visit to America at his invitation. As the first president of the American Psychological Association, with a white beard and dark eyebrows framing a squinting eye, Hall taught a hybrid of unrepentant eugenics that preached that schools should exist to indoctrinate military discipline, a love of authority, an awe of nature, and a devotion to the state. But while Hall has been mainly relegated to now-forgotten leather-bound volumes, his remaining fame hangs stubbornly from a single peg: an 1895 study he oversaw titled *Of Peculiar and Exceptional Children.* The deficiencies of the only child, according to his conclusion, are no less than an unassailable, eminently verifiable rule of nature. As he wrote, "it will be noticed that creatures which have large families, whether beasts or birds, have less trouble in rearing them than those which have only one or two young. Little pigs are weeks ahead of young calves, and the young partridge, with its dozen brothers and sisters, is far more teachable than the young eagle."

Raised in a Rockwellian scrum of siblings in rural Massachusetts, Hall looked back on his own pastoral childhood with eyes damp with nostalgia. Like many of us, he believed that what worked for him must work for everyone else. Furthermore, the converse was true: alternatives to his big-brood happiness were suspect. And though there was no scientific measurement of any kind beyond his work, Hall's authority made it so. Even more than his own fame or a network to disseminate his work, it may have been Hall's language of absolutes that made his conclusions so permanently written in our collective understanding. At the end of a 1907 lecture about how singletons are sickly, selfish, strange, and stupid, Hall simply concluded: "Being an only child is a disease in itself."

"Politicians, not scientists, spout hypotheses—make proclamations without testing—and then move on to the next one. That's what Stanley Hall did," science historian and evolutionary psychologist Frank Sulloway tells me. Sulloway spends a great deal of time thinking about Charles Darwin and family formation in his office at the University of California, Berkeley, where photographs from the Galapagos Islands hang above the Eastern Mountain Sports frame pack he carried on his first voyage there forty years ago. He believes a Darwinian impetus may well underlie the stereotype because our relatives had an evolutionary imperative to spread their own genes. "They need a good story to convince us to do this. So they say, 'Have just one and it'll come out rotten,'" Sulloway says. Then again, he adds that Darwinian interests could also tell us "you're better off investing in a small number of offspring; larger families are no longer adaptive."

It wasn't just Hall supporting the notion that parents of only children are responsible for producing "rotten" kids. A cottage industry of parenting literature, in books and periodicals, sprung up in the fallow provinces of his child study movement. The wisdom of the Abel sisters, Elsie C. and Theodora Mead, argued in their 1926 *The Guide to Good Manners for Kids*, that as a parents' "chief concern," an only child is bound to be a "spoiled child," with apparently shameful behavior—not that the Abel sisters cite any research to this effect. Two married speech therapists, Smiley and Margaret Gray Blanton, offered even more damning—but no more scientific—conclusions in the 1927 issue of *Child Guidance*. "The only child is greatly handicapped. He cannot be expected to go through life with the same capacity for adjustment that the child reared in the family with other children has," they write, adding that the singleton is forever stunted, as "the only way in which he can exceed these adults is in infantile behavior. He can scream, louder than they can. He can throw himself on the floor." Bad manners indeed.

Infantile behavior has nothing on how Viennese neuropsychiatrist—and former Alfred Adler protégé—Erwin Wexberg diagnosed only children in his 1927 book *Your Nervous Child:* "For the most part, such children have a boundless egotism, they tyrannize over their friends and will suffer no gods beside themselves." (Now read it again in an Austrian accent and tell me *you* don't feel like a nervous child.) Such denunciations weren't simply found in parenting books by so-called professionals, but in the popular press. An article on only children in *Liberty* magazine that same year, featuring an illustration of a child on a throne with a scepter in his hand, discussed how only children are late to walk and talk, lack initiative, think the world "owes them a living," are overly negative and fearful, crave undue sympathy, and are finicky eaters and hypochondriacs.

But in 1928, a researcher named Norman Fenton tested the Hall hypothesis and published his findings in *The Pedagogical Seminary and Journal of Genetic Psychology*. Not content to leave such assumptions to the press, Fenton asked a university class in child psychology to briefly describe their psychological assessment of only children. Out of fifty students, only two thought singletons "were in any regard normal." The rest gave the usual litany of stereotypes, "some even going so far as to state that they could pick them out at sight!" he wrote. Fenton's point was clear— this was not merely a case of public alarmism, but an assumption held even by students in a university environment dedicated to challenging such assumptions from a clinical perspective. In the lecture hall and general public alike, a unanimous verdict had been levied against the neurotic despots in their midst. And so Fenton set out to do the first actual testing of the assumption, providing teachers with detailed questionnaires to gather statistical data about all their students—onlies and siblings alike—just as researchers do today.

What he discovered should have buried the myth right there. Fenton found that in measures of generosity and sociability, "two traits in which in ordinary accounts only children were supposed to be inferior," he wrote, only children tested more favorably than kids with siblings. They were more likely to be truthful. They showed greater initiative, leadership abilities, and self-assuredness. According to teachers asked to assess "nervous symptoms" of their students, the worst sufferers were youngest children (about half), then oldest (just over forty percent), then middle children (just under forty percent), with just thirty-two percent of only children demonstrating the thriving "nervous manifestations" described by Erwin Wexler. In adding intelligence tests to the mix,

Fenton found that singletons scored highest. It's true that they were a little less obedient than their larger-family cohort. Some teachers, he wrote, believed only children to be more aggressive and conceited; otherwise, he found no difference between kids raised without siblings and children from a fuller house.

But no one listened. There were no Fenton Clubs to spread his findings, even as additional research confirmed his results. That same year, two studies published in the *Journal of Genetic Psychology* found similar assets to onliness: one said they were more gregarious than kids with siblings, and another said they had fewer behavior problems in school.

As the press warned decent citizens of the dark menace of singletons in their midst, the country collapsed into the Great Depression. Like in any major economic crisis, fertility sunk along with the stock market. In a statistical analysis of the modern family in the 1932 *ANNALS of the American Academy of Political and Social Science*, Yale's Mildred Parten observed that among those families containing children, "the one-child family predominates." Within just a few years, the number of single child homes in the United States rose to more than thirty percent.

Yet the alarm kept ringing. In *Good Housekeeping*, Josephine Hemenway Kenyon, director of the Health and Happiness Club, wrote a stern column called "Plan Your Family Wisely," illustrated by a photograph of a lone screaming child. "Let this be a plea," she wrote, "if a one-child home, for the advent of a second baby." In such trying times, having a second child takes no less than "pioneer courage," Kenyon told readers. And the danger was not simply that you'd raise miserably flawed offspring—a single-child family could also prove poisonous to adults, as "either the parent or the child, sooner or later, will present behavior problems." By

1936, only children were so common, and so commonly damned, that an advice columnist in the *Christian Science Monitor* answered a letter from a concerned parent of a troubled kid by saying, "Perhaps it happens that you have but one child, an only child, that much-quoted and much-abused statement and problem!"

It wasn't until 1942 that a defense of the only child began to emerge in the press. That's when *The New York Times* published a story titled "Kind Words for the 'Only' Child," an aggregation of the full shelf of research dismantling Hall's hypotheses that had emerged since Norman Fenton's study. The "common assumption that the only child is apt to be a selfish and unsocial brat, handicapped by his solitary status and by too much parental coddling" was nothing but a ball of gas, the article said. And yet, hundreds of studies later, that assumption lived on, here and abroad. In a 1977 survey, seventy-six percent of Americans still said they thought that being an only child was a serious disadvantage in life, responsible for everything from gutting loneliness to major character defects.

And that was (and is) hardly just an American point of view. When, in 1987, twenty-seven-year-old Michael Ryan shot thirty-one people in Hungerford, England, before killing himself, the British press asserted "the usual overattention of a single child," rather than crippling mental illness, made the man a murderer. (Eric Harris and Dylan Klebold both had siblings, if you're wondering, but the fictional adolescent single shooter in *We Need to Talk About Kevin* is a singleton.) The next year the UK magazine *Today* authoritatively announced that social life is a "minefield" for the "lonely" only—"growing up with the idea that they are at the center of the universe, it is almost impossible for them to shake off their selfishness, and it shows."

In 1990, in the midst of such public singleton damnation, English researcher Ann Laybourn cataloged the singleton stereotype in the press and tested the profile, just like Norman Fenton did in the twenties. Like investigators before her, she found that "despite the fact that they tended to come from less advantaged backgrounds only children performed similarly or slightly better than those from two child families on behavioral and educational measures," she wrote in *Children & Society*.

Laybourn noticed that the British press treatment of China's only children was astonishing in its complete acceptance of the stereotype. *The Guardian* published a 1986 story on Chinese "fat brats," contending that the population of Sino-singletons are "indulgent, selfish, introverted, unconcerned and unable to care for themselves"—adding *obese* to the disproven *lonelyselfishmaldjusted* trope. A *Sunday Times* story headlined "China's Brat Pack: Generation of Only-Children" predicts "the behavioral time bomb" to come: "a China in the early 21st century full of selfish and dictatorial young adults." But perhaps most startling is another *Times* article that discusses the horrors of forced abortion and infanticide only to conclude, "but the problems China is experiencing now are minor compared with the problems that could emerge in the future . . . with difficult only children."

The stereotype was surely helped along internationally by the invention of the term "Little Emperor," which began as a *Newsweek* headline on March 13, 1985, seven years after China introduced the One Child Policy. This derogatory summation of China's one hundred million singletons was embraced instantly as pure fact around the world. I had to explain what a Little Emperor was during many interviews in China—it hasn't entered their discourse as it has ours—but once I did, they knew just what I meant. In my travels there, I heard frequently, "Yes, they are all selfish like an emperor!" underscored with a big smile of recognition.

Just as sinister as the stereotype of the selfish only child is the stereotype of the selfish parent of one. Some of us consider the choice to stop at one due to preference, others due to need. Regardless, just like the only children we bear, we end up vilified. Consider Oscar Wilde's philosophy: "Selfishness is not living as one wishes to live, it is asking others to live as one wishes to live." If I choose not to give my daughter the sibling the world believes she is owed—whether or not she wants one—that means I am asking her to live as I wish her to live. This is true. But is it really selfish?

As author Catherine Carswell pronounced in *Fortnightly* in 1933, it's "a wretched woman who has no children, but the more pitiable object [is] the married woman who has only one child." Parents of only children are "deliberate malingerers," she wrote, rampant in a society of increasingly common single-child families. "The faults of the mother of one," she added, "are notorious in our tradition." Carswell's anxiety, and that of countless others, was perhaps twofold. What would a woman be if she were more than a mother? And if the right sort of women weren't having larger families, who would? This was the age of eugenics, an era of pronounced and ugly racial panic. In 1936's *Science News Letter*, Columbia professor John C. Flanagan warned, "The best part of the population's intellectual abilities, economic talents, and physical health are losing out numerically while the less desirable biologically are gradually peopling the nations." Why? The high price of raising children, he wrote, was causing families to greatly

limit their family size, especially in "matters important to professional men and their wives" such as insurance, housing, child care,
and the steep cost of college tuitions. But when Gallup pollsters
asked average citizens why they thought parents were opting for
onlies, leisure and snobbery were the main reasons cited.

"Everyone wants to be uppish and not have more kids," said
one respondent. "Couples like to gad about and won't take the
time to raise children," jibed another. Only twenty percent of parents polled about their own choices agreed with the notion that
"youngsters interfere with parents' freedom." Mainly people simply said they didn't know how they could afford more children.
But the role was cast. As sure as the singleton was inarguably
selfish, so was the parent of one. And as the party foisting what
Carswell called "the long misery of their childish years" onto a
powerless daughter or son, parental selfishness deserved to be exposed and condemned.

In 1955, *The Milbank Memorial Fund Quarterly* published a
study on the social and psychological factors leading to stopping
at one, which at least offered some research to complicate the
parental stereotype, even if it's unlikely many people read it. In it,
Lois Pratt and P. K. Whipton surveyed 1,444 "relatively fecund"
couples, many of whom who had opted out of a second child.
Their reasons feel quite familiar. The couples said they could not
afford more children; they cited health reasons and housing difficulties, and many said their "parental instincts [had been] satisfied with children already born." Furthermore, they discovered
that nearly half of parents who planned to stop at one said they
liked their child "very much" (on a scale of very much, much,
some, or little)—twice as many as parents of two kids. (Under
five percent of parents with three children liked their kids "very

much.") And couples who said they planned to stop at one were reportedly more "interested" in their kids than parents of siblings. Pratt and Whipton offered this analysis of their results: "The norm may encourage couples to have a second child who, on the basis of their low level of liking for children, would be inclined to have only one child." In other words, parents who chose to stop at one weren't selfish. They didn't hate kids. And they didn't make the choice because they were broke. They were usually just happy with the one child they already had. This finding hardly made headlines, but it predicted a shift soon to come.

The boned bodices of the fifties gave way to the liberated sixties, with the feminist seventies finally emerging from cultural upheaval. A 1972 feature in *The New York Times Magazine* called "Choosing to Stop at One," framed by advertisements for sectional couches and ski vacations (the graphic design equivalent of an eight-track tape), connected family size and the new liberated woman. "Increasing numbers of women are coming to feel that they can realize their other ambitions in life and still enjoy the experience of motherhood by having a one child family," journalist Rita Kramer wrote. She interviewed Margaret Mead: "Well, I always wanted six children," Mead said. "But life worked out in such a way that I only had one. Today, however, I'd have just one" she says, as an ideal and not just as a compromise. The article is heavy with the intent to overthrow the mantle of the parent-of-one as pathologically self-centered and replace it with the language of liberation. Or, as Kramer quoted Dr. E. James Lieberman, "The problem" is not choosing to stop at one, but "the idea people have that they should either have no children or two as a minimum. This is deplorable. We have to make delayed parenthood and the one-child family respectable." The next year my mother would become pregnant with me.

Anne Roiphe carried the cause in the same publication several years later, in 1977, when my mother reached the "advanced maternal age" of her midthirties, and when environmental panic, nuclear armament, and a new cadre of briefcase-toting women had entered the culture in full force. Roiphe wrote, "Images of man's future that have us standing on our one square foot of allotted space or waiting on infinite lines for a cup of desalinated water; women's newfound drive for self-realization, for doctoral degrees and executive secretaries of their own; concern about holocaust, revolution, depression—these cause many young couples to pause before conceiving a second child." If that sentence could have fit on a button, I have no doubt many women in the seventies would have pinned it on with pride. A decade prior only six percent of parents admitted to planning to stop at one—by the time Roiphe's article was published, that number had shot up to seventeen percent.

But that didn't mean their plans found much societal support. Many of these women likely remember their own version of the nursery school showdown my mother endured, briefcase in hand, when more traditional mothers were appalled at the choice to make oneself an equal priority to one's child. As T. Berry Brazelton wrote in *Redbook* in 1979—the year my mother, convinced she was pregnant, sat up all night on the couch, writing pros and cons lists as the sun rose—"in a way though it is easier to give in to a decision to have a second than to stand firm in one's wish to only have one child." The moment had arrived to begin accepting the only child, and the parent who said *one and done*.

In *Glamour* in 1982—around the time my mother started saying to me, "When you are a mother, should you ever choose to be one"—Marcia Kamien published an essay on how she grew up without siblings and turned out just fine. It's not the content of her story I found most revealing, but rather the advertisement for the Equal Rights Amendment that shared the page. It said: "In 1960, 52 percent of all women were employed as clericals, saleswomen, and hairdressers. In 1979, 47 percent of all working women were still in these low-paying jobs." The ERA failed in Congress. The possibility of policy initiatives attempting to reconcile motherhood with modernity was dead in the water. Ours is the political culture that remains, which leaves the reasons parents stop at one just as Lois Pratt and P. K. Whipton found them in their study decades before. Housing. Insurance. Child care. Education. Plus, something we'll never need policy to address: feeling satisfied with just the one we already love. But just as the notion of state support for middle-class parenting was an aberration of an era, so was the possibility that our culture could accept the one-and-done approach as a legitimate ethical choice.

It happens on the subway, at restaurants, on busy street corners. If you have just one kid, it's happened to you. It's not just relatives who have internalized the myth, it's complete strangers. This time it happens when Dahlia and I are buying milk at the supermarket. The cashiers fawn over her pink cheeks and applaud when she twirls for them, and then I endure this typical dialogue:

"Your first?"

"Yup."

"Another one coming soon?"

"It might be just this one."

"You'll have more. You'll see."

"At the moment, I'm not planning on it."

"You wouldn't do that to your child. You'll see."

I was astonished to learn that the prejudice against only children and their parents extends beyond the supermarket—and the family reunion—and onto the therapist's couch. It turns out that acceptance of the stereotype remains common among psychologists, exactly the people who should know better themselves and be helping others to know better too. So says one educational psychologist and researcher named Adriean Mancillas. Mancillas is an only child; so is her husband. The Southern California couple intended to stop at one child themselves—they are among the three percent of Americans who have told Gallup pollsters recently that the single child family is their ideal. (Their one-and-done pregnancy, it turned out, yielded triplets.)

Mancillas studies the stereotyping of only children and has become exceedingly aware of how social judgment extends to parents of singletons as well. Her interest was not just spurred by her own past, but by a paper she encountered a few years ago: "Some quasi-academic writing," from a teacher's point of view, she says, about how educators worry that singletons in a classroom will monopolize time because they're so attention seeking. "There was no peer review behind this piece—nothing. But it opened my eyes to how pervasive the stereotype of only children can be even in written material for professionals," she says.

Sociologist Judith Blake observed the same issue in the eighties when she wrote in *Family Size and Achievement*, "The belief that being an only child is a significant handicap appears to be so generally accepted that academic psychologists suggest it is a 'cultural truism,'" despite the copious research to the contrary. This erroneous thinking—from professionals—continues into the current day. One educational psychologist who writes about single-child families won't even use the words "only child" in her papers, because she considers it a derogatory term, even in profes-sional circles. Just a few years ago, psychologist Alan E. Stewart at the University of Georgia found that clinicians believed only children are "particularly likely to experience problems." And in a paper on biased clinical judgment in *Journal of Counseling and Development*, he described therapists discussing hypothetical cli-ents in terms of negative singleton mythology.

Fueled by the belief that this tendency warps the treatment only children and their families receive, Mancillas set out to ex-amine the literature on singleton stereotypes with an eye toward alerting her colleagues. She found that from Estonia, to Korea, to the Netherlands, the *lonelyselfishmaladjusted* bias is the same. "Why would it be the same story in Brazil as it is in the US? It's the same underpinning: Bigger families were needed to farm the land. Plus we share the same evolutionary psychology," she tells me.

Only children share that psychology as well. The perception of the corrupted and disadvantaged singleton, it turns out, runs through the collective singleton bloodstream. In scouring studies globally from the past three decades, Mancillas found a theme cropping up across the research. In studies that were replicated in 1985, 1993, and 2003, parents of only children, adult singletons, and groups of college students all agreed that as a group "only chil-dren are the most academic and spoiled and the least likable." But when asked about individuals—in the case of parents, their child, and in the case of adult onlies, themselves—they had different responses. Individuals ranked completely outside that assessment. In other words, *not my kid, not me*. Mancillas found only children and their parents internalize the stereotype, no matter how they refute it within their own families. Or as two researchers in Hol-land described in an article on the "Well-Being of Only Children" in *Adolescence*, only children are "regarded with pity and distrust," which is no doubt wounding. The effect of the stereotype, they write, will hurt parents as well, "leaving them with a sense of guilt, which may complicate the relationship with their child."

Mancillas also learned that stereotypes of parents of only children are equally enduring. One 1989 survey of parents themselves found that most believed that "even when people consider that most only children may indeed possess positive characteristics, the tendency exists for them to dismiss such strengths as emanating from an environment that is overly indulgent." Plus, parents of only children say in general—*not me!*—that they are overprotecting and smothering, according to another study that year.

Once types like this are set, no one wants to undo them, Mancillas says. "It's not like racial stereotyping, which you can demonstrate is really dangerous for people, so we've had to address it. With only children, there's no impetus to weaken the belief." What other stereotype survived political correctness unscathed? Singleton prejudice is the lone cockroach scuttling across the postnuclear landscape the nineties left behind. In the case of every group of people I can think of, every subculture, every ethnicity, nearly every diagnosis—from middle children to Inuits to sexual masochists—the culture has recognized and rejected the bias. On television, *Glee* may have cast every type of kid who could possibly, ever, maybe be a victim of bias (the gay kid! the stuttering Korean girl! the dude in the wheelchair!). But there's only one character who represents Hall's fantasy of the only child, the widely despised, arrogant, self-obsessed Rachel. In one episode Rachel loses her voice. Her reaction? This adenoidal whine: "Who am I without my voice? I'm just another spoiled annoying only child."

"From what the research says," Mancillas tells me, "it's just the same now as ever—as it was in the Stanley Hall days." And as is the case with the cognitive social psychology behind all bias maintenance, people seek out examples that confirm their belief and ignore what refutes it. Ann Laybourn, the British researcher who put the cultural bias to the Fenton test, wondered what inner holy grail was granting immortality to this myth. Here's a theory she proffered: "Bad news is better news than good news," she wrote. "Happy only children will not think the fact worth mentioning, and therefore the complaints of those who've had a poor experience will predominate."

Someone needs to be the scapegoat for the disappointments of the plentiful nuclear family: parenting more than one kid is simply too hard to not be supported by some dogma that it's for a higher good, *for the children*. "It is obviously not very cheering to believe that these sacrifices have been in vain, and that only children whose parents have had it easier have turned out all right," Laybourn wrote. To reduce the discomfort of this possibility, she says, "the idea develops that only children must be disadvantaged in some other way; they have more possessions and attention so they must be spoiled; they avoid conflicts with siblings so they must be lonely." Of course, we all know what the worst thing is about the parents of only children. It's not how terribly they parent; it's that they only had one kid in the first place. They didn't muster the moral fortitude and "pioneer courage" to breed again.

Adriean Mancillas offers that as one method to relieve some of that pressure to have a second child, family planning clinics would disseminate the idea that only children are just fine, thank you. That's in addition to her advocacy, via research, in fighting the stereotype in a clinical environment. I wish her luck: Sorenson, the British psychologist who wrote *Only Child and Adulthood*, tells me that in a professional setting, "I can spot the only child in the first couple of hours." She adds, "If we have problems with anyone, it's the only child without fail," even if five hundred-odd quantitative studies tell us otherwise.

TWO

RHYMES WITH ONLY

I s one really the loneliest number? I've heard it hundreds of times now, in countless interviews and cocktail party conversations: our fear of conferring onliness is mainly about sentencing a kid to loneliness. It's articulated in myriad ways. *I want her to have a teammate. He needs someone who can be on his side. She has to have a sibling to play with. Who will be there for him when I'm gone?* At the root of most every parent's—or future parent's—anxiety about having an only child is a visceral response to the notion of that child *alone.*

It may be true, as Thomas Wolfe wrote, that "loneliness is and always has been the central and inevitable experience of every man," but we tend to see it amplified in the experience of the only child. In many languages the word "only" not only means "solo" but also "alone," and according to an etymological dictionary, "now usual in reference to emotional states." "Only" dates back to Old English, whereas "lonely" entered the lexicon during the Renaissance, but the words have become poignantly synonymous.

Fear of loneliness is not some neurotic modern invention. Our survival long depended on the tribe, the community. Social pain evolved as a way of alerting us to the danger of isolation. For hundreds of years, people have wondered if there is a physical component to loneliness, expressed in a smell—a physical condition with olfactory symptoms, a potential contagion.

Happiness is most often understood as the absence of loneliness. When talking about what gives them the deepest pleasure and comfort, people always rank intimacy, love, and social affiliation at the top of the list. A University of Michigan survey found that one fifth of people considered loneliness to be the deepest source of unhappiness in their lives. And such unhappiness is more common than ever. Recently, researchers at Duke found that in 1985 most people counted at least three friends as close confidantes; in 2004 most people could name only two. Even more dramatically, the number of people who felt they did not have a single person with whom to discuss important matters tripled to almost a quarter of Americans surveyed.

We pity the lonely adults among us—the woman alone in a restaurant, the man alone at the movies. But we at least might ascribe what we perceive as their loneliness to a series of life choices. The toddler alone in the sandbox seizes our hearts in a different way. We can't imagine he has any say in the matter. Nor can we imagine that he might actually be perfectly happy.

Being alone and being lonely are not synonymous—not in the least. One is an objective state; the other is a subjective experience. We often mistake loneliness with solitude, confusing a state of grievous misery with a state of placid contentment, the likes of Thoreau's exaltations or the teachings of Buddhism. One can be alone among others, isolated à la *The Lonely Crowd*, or inhabiting the anguished loneliness of an unhappy twosome. Or one can know the inimitable joy of a day spent with no company but a novel, under the covers in a delicious fortress of solitude. "Loneliness is the poverty of self; solitude is the richness of self," May Sarton wrote—a musing that makes me want to pull on a coat, leave behind my cell phone, and take an indulgently long walk on a crisp day.

Of course, the fact that I thrill to the notion of solitude, though I can be one of the most obsessively social people I know, may be testament to my own onliness, which I, for one, have rarely experienced as loneliness. When Toni Falbo and her colleague Denise Polit conducted a meta-analysis of 115 studies comparing only children with siblings, examining surveys that were both self-reported and measuring the perceptions of others, they found that onlies score no higher on loneliness than anyone else. Furthermore, only children report less of a need for social affiliation than others.

An Austin-based psychologist named Carl Pickhardt, who wrote an excellent book called *The Future of Your Only Child: How to Guide Your Child to a Happy and Successful Life*, says that one of the "gifts" of only childhood is being "a good companion for yourself." He explains, "Only children are well self-connected in their primary relationship in their life." By primary relationship, what he means is that whether we like it or not, married or single, identical twin or only child, every relationship we have is secondary to the one we have with ourselves—*nowhere to run to, baby, nowhere to hide*. It helps to like to hang out with the one you can never quit. Echoing the observations of many psychologists and researchers, and drawing from years of observation and analysis in his practice rather than quantitative research, Pick-hardt has found that "time alone, far from being painful, becomes rewarding because the only child is establishing a bond of last-ing benefit—a primary friendship with himself," he says. "This bond creates a foundation of self-sufficiency that contributes to the only child's independence, an enjoyment of solitude, and an affirmative relationship to himself."

Denyse, an adult singleton in Iowa, tells me, "I've always been a loner. I guess it's the only-child thing. I'm not going to invite friends over to chat. I'm very selective. I'd rather watch TV or read a book. I'm just happier just me." Denyse wrote her college thesis on woman video gamers. Now she runs a day-care center and is married to a man who works nights at an aluminum fac-tory. "I only see him for a total of an hour a day. Works great for me, other than wanting more help around the house. I can't say I'm lonely. Classic only child, I'm telling you," she says. That's cer-tainly one way of developing an understanding of oneself. But I'd love to sit her down with Kisha, in Buffalo, who says, "I'm always social, always entertaining, always surrounded by friends, which I've always attributed to being an only child."

Often when I meet singletons with seemingly opposite per-sonalities and habits, they ascribe their most striking elements, no matter what they are, to their lack of siblings. Onliness becomes a totalizing narrative—the thing that defines us, that makes sense of us, that overwhelms the other factors that shape us.

Vanessa and her husband, Mike, in Rochester, New York, represent both ends of the spectrum in one relationship. Vanessa met her stepbrother for the first time when she was sixteen; Mike has two half siblings who were in their twenties when he was born; each grew up without a brother or sister in the house. "You could say we're both typical only children in our own way," Vanessa tells me, "but my husband couldn't be any more different from me, especially socially." She's never known a man who talks on the phone as much as he does—"I'm not talking about work, I'm talking about just talking with his guy friends all the time"— while she is content to pick up the phone maybe once a week to check in with her best friend. "I'm always saying to him, 'Who are you?' Why do you need to be in touch with everybody all the time?'" Vanessa says their friends are really his friends. He's the social connector, and she's the reticent one. "I'm a real skeptic about people. I hold back when I meet anyone. I assume I'm not going to get along with people." She tells me she lets Mike do all the talking, and before she knows it, they've got some new friends. "If it wasn't for him, I'd have my one close friend—other than him, he's really my best friend—and I'd be fine, but he needs this, and I'm happy for him to have it. We're different strands of only children, I guess," which she says is exactly why she thinks they're so well matched.

We can be happy along the spectrum of solitude, blissfully rattling around the house alone, reading and lost in our meandering thoughts and then swinging to a different set of needs, racing out of the house for a mind-melding conversation with a confidante or joining friends for a boisterous afternoon. Or we can feel caught between both poles, never satisfied with our present reality, always wondering what we might be missing in ourselves and in the company of others. Everyone can—and does—feel this, not just only children.

But for onlies it might feel more acute. Emiliano in Chico, California, is constantly questioning his relationship with himself and his connection with others. He tells me he can be alone a great deal and has always been comfortable on his own, and yet he feels like he's always had a really poor relationship with himself. "Sometimes I look at people talking to each other with deep eye contact and wonder if they're having a level of relationship I don't have," he says. "I crave deep relationship—not just with myself but with others. Often I don't achieve it, but often I do. Still, I mainly get hung up on when I don't."

This craving tends to be pronounced in only children, which a range of researchers say accounts for the fact that only children, contrary to popular assumption, actually tend to be more adept at forging connections than other people. John Cacioppo, who heads up the Center for Cognitive Neuroscience at the University of Chicago, and who coauthored, with William Patrick, *Loneliness: Human Nature and the Need for Social Connection*, tells me only children are especially hungry for connection, and thus are unusually attuned to the responsibility that comes with building lasting relationships. Cacioppo says he thinks our strong primary relationship with ourselves is a bit beside the point. Being alone, he says, tends to not be the principal experience of only children. Instead, he says, "The solitary childhood isn't actually solitary—it exquisitely conditions you for a social life."

Or as Jacqueline Olds, a psychiatrist who was an only child until age ten, who coauthored the book *The Lonely American: Drifting Apart in the Twenty-first Century*, puts it, "You learn to keep yourself good company, but you also tend to connect more intimately and profoundly with other people." Sure, she says, there's all the "internal chatting with oneself" that we tend to do—and she says that's good for us—but it only goes so far. "We all have an urge to compare notes. If you don't have a sibling to compare notes with, you find people," she says. "In my own life,

I was hungry for connection, so I took friends on as sisters." I
certainly did this. I do this still.

My life has been a succession of intense friendships. The closest
ones have lacked boundaries, sometimes gloriously so, sometimes
tortuously so, with often-constant contact. I'm fortunate that my
marriage has accommodated these deep intimacies—with men
as well as women—rarely at a cost. Many of these friends are
only children themselves, in search of the same fierce connection
I've craved. Others have siblings, with whom some are close, and
some are not. "What we share most of all is that we're intimacy
junkies," comments my friend Eric—a younger brother himself.

First there was Leah, who I played with after school and every
weekend. We were small girls with giant imaginations, inhabiting cavernous, craggy worlds of fairies and demons. My freckles,
her braids inseparable—unless her older sister was around, whom
I worshipped and who would steal away my attention, sending
Leah to sulk in her room. Later there was Laura, an only herself, whom I would call as soon as I got home from spending
the day at school with her, continuing our conversation as we
had left it ten minutes before. The once-coiled kitchen telephone
cord was straightened from the daily hours it was pulled down
the hall and around my doorframe to reach my bed. We'd hang
up when parents came home for dinner, only to dial again during
approved hours—watching *Moonlighting* on the phone together
every Tuesday night—until my parents laid down some law.

On the first day of high school, I met Sarah. She was wearing
Body Glove leggings and a formidable amount of hair spray—
my later-life friends know her as "Aerosmith Sarah," not a name
I ever conferred on her—while my closet was stocked with a

vintage leopard coat and platform boots. Sarah's hockey habit never conflicted with my literary leanings. We were like sisters—though she has an unusually close one of her own—with each our own tastes and tendencies, yet sharing the same secret language. One of her boyfriends once commented that witnessing us talk together was like watching a "spastic mental Rolodex" flip through its cards on warp speed. Twenty-odd years later, we still call ourselves this, a spastic mental Rolodex. And despite conflicts, misunderstandings, and periods of separation, we still use the same shorthand. When we need to, Sarah and I talk every day. But most of the time we don't.

She's has come to understand that I need time to simply be left alone in what Carl Pickhardt would call my primary relationship. ("You're a disappearer," an only-child friend said to me recently. "I understand. I'm a disappearer too. I think it's one of those things we tend to have in common.") And Sarah understands I need other intimacy junkies in my life too. She's seen decades of dear friends come and sometimes go. Some of them I still count as family, some I lost along the way, some I lost and found again.

In my journey among only children all over the world, I've heard most people describe the same cascade of intimates I have known. My friend Anya, who grew up in Berkeley, California, attaches herself with the same ferocity I do—when she lived around the corner from me, we'd end up at my dining table together several times a week, just as she's done with other friends since she was a kid. Judy, growing up in Manhattan in the seventies, had a deep network of best friends who through college were all singletons themselves. Marta, who was born in northern Poland and immigrated to the United States thirty years ago as a child, had four best friends growing up, three of them only children, all of them like sisters. Mads, in Berlin, lives in a walk-up filled with other onlies, most of whom end up in his living room after school. Eleanor, in Brooklyn Heights, knows the family down the hall will leave their door unlocked all evening in case she wants to push it open and see their daughter, her best friend, after dinner. In Xuhua's apartment complex in Beijing, kids have the unattended run of the courtyard.

You'll notice my above litany of onlies with close intimates are all urbanites. My best friends were all within walking distance when I was a kid, and when I was stuck at home, my friend Jonathan was just three floors above me. Without parents perennially available to spend their free hours as a suburban car service, the social contact I often reached for as a kid is harder to access. Patricia Nachman, a psychologist who wrote the book *You and Your Only Child*, says this proximity is the main factor in how connected kids can feel: "It's simply different in the city or the country, I mean, totally different if you're together with other kids in the projects, say, or living in a house with no one around for twenty miles. Who on earth are you going to play with?"

Those divisions between city kids and their carpooling counterparts become more extreme and more common, creeping from farmland into the front yards of suburbia. An essayist in England a few years ago measured the radius of where his grandfather was free to roam (the pond, miles away), compared to where his father could claim as his territory (the farthest reaches of the neighborhood), compared to where he was allowed to wander (the end of the block), compared to the gate enclosing his front garden, which is as far as his own child is permitted to play unattended. As a kid's locus of free rein shrinks radically, so do the

numbers of children therein, and the opportunities to connect to
a world bigger than oneself.

Dean, now in his forties, agrees to talk to me because, as he
says with a sly grin, "being an only child is a fate I wouldn't wish
on my worst enemy." When I challenge him, he admits he means
specifically his experience of only childhood growing up lonely
and only in a small town—three hundred people small—on the
rural border of New Jersey and Pennsylvania. With specifically
his parents. "My sense memory of childhood was being isolated
and sad," he tells me. His parents were disinterested in him and
would boast, "Dean takes care of himself." He did: he would draw
silently for hours while his parents entertained their friends in
the other room. Then, when Dean was eight, his parents split up,
his mother moved two hours away, and he spent his weekends
shuttling back and forth between homes. All that driving was
in the service of shared custody, not to take him to visit a friend,
so he doesn't remember really having any. "I almost felt like an
orphan," he tells me—though without the camaraderie of an or-
phanage. Then, at age sixteen, Dean enrolled in Bard College at
Simon's Rock in the Berkshires, and his utter social disconnection came to an abrupt and relieving end. There, awaiting him,
were the intense relationships he had long desired.

It's tough raising a kid in the best circumstances, and I admit
I have some empathy for a parent who has to meet a child's social needs in the sticks. In Brooklyn, I can spontaneously take
Dahlia down the block to play dress-up (while I drink wine in
the kitchen with her friend's mother). That's not the case for a
whole population of single-child families. Debi, a child psychologist in rural Missouri, doesn't have any concerns about raising an
only child, save for geographic ones. Her family history is one of

formidable fertility—her great-aunt bought a used school bus to cart around her fourteen kids, her father was one of nine, and her mother was one of six. By comparison Debi and her three siblings felt like a small brood. "But I would have gladly given every one of my siblings away—there's a reason I became a child psychologist," she confesses over coffee. Her long gray hair drapes over the shoulder of her red long-sleeve shirt; she and her daughter are dressed as twins today. When at age forty-one Debi adopted Sarah from China, she didn't think twice. But now that Sarah is three, she's acutely aware of her daughter's isolation. It's a quarter mile to the end of their driveway, and a half mile to the nearest next youngest person for miles, who is seventeen years old. Sarah "can't go out and play in the neighborhood, because we have no neighborhood," she tells me.

Though Sarah has friends from the day care she attends, frankly, Debi admits, what it takes to pull off a play date feels impossible. "My time is never enough to cover such distance," Debi says. It's a minimum hour in the car round trip to a birthday party, usually much more. "It's a lot at the end of a long week." So they end up spending weekends running errands, going out to dinner, or watching football on television, without another kid in sight. Sarah's nearest cousin is in St. Louis; the one she likes most lives in California. Last week, when it was her favorite cousin's birthday, they baked a cake and ate it in her honor, two thousand miles away.

Debi tells me she's been thinking about how to create a community for Sarah online, if she can't deliver one in person down their gravel road. Patricia Nachman believes the intimacy that develops between kids online can be both rich and positive. Furthermore, she told me she thinks that it has transformed the culture of home, and "equalized the territory between onlies and siblings," she says. "Even when there are siblings at home, they aren't talking to their siblings, they're texting their friends. It's changed everything." My after-school phone calls with Laura were a precursor to this virtual intimacy. I know what a difference it made, even from the standpoint of my minimal eighties tech level of contact, nothing compared to what's possible in our wired age.

Nachman says texting and email allow for deep personal connection, but others aren't so sure. The prefrontal cortex receives information from all five senses, and the more senses are engaged, the richer the connection, the more social cohesion is fostered. Email, however, is what's known as a single-strand interaction. It engages our sight, but nothing else. There exist only words on a screen, no texture, no tone, no body language. Nothing develops connection as richly as in-person contact. We look for physical cues from another person when we seek connection with them—mannerisms, posture, expressions—and so human bonding is less satisfying without bodies and faces to read.

The online world allows only children to feel just as connected as kids with siblings at home, and in closer touch with their friends than any of us have ever been—so says *Drifting Apart in the Twenty-first Century* author Jacqueline Olds. "Only children now have people to compare notes with at any time, for the first time. You weren't in a position when you could call up your best friend at one a.m."—not that I didn't sometimes—"but today you could send an instant message at that hour without even thinking about it"—and I do, even now. But Olds says that isn't always a good thing. "A thousand IMs coming in doesn't give you a sense of well-being, it just makes you feel souped up, more wired," she says. "When you're typing away, you're not truly relating." In fact, Olds believes the feeling of always being available makes people "more terrified of being alone." We have lost the ability to keep ourselves company, she says—a crucial mechanism for only children, as well as what Pickhardt considers our greatest gift. To rephrase Olds's thinking, we've not only lost the richness of connection, we've lost the richness of solitude.

Solitude is something that twelve-year-old Maya in Canton, Georgia, has plenty of. She's an only child, and she's homeschooled by her mother. Her closest friend, Allie, lives in Tampa. They met a couple of years ago, and their relationship exists almost exclusively online. A few days a week they Skype. "We talk as if we're coming home from school together," Maya tells me, though she not only has to imagine what coming home with Allie would be like, she has to imagine what coming home from school would be like, period. Her closest cousins are in Nashville and Charlotte—"We're like sisters and brothers," she says—but they primarily communicate online as well. When I meet Maya and her parents, her father pipes up that Maya has friends in their neighborhood, and at church on Sundays she sees "church friends," none of whom anyone in the family can easily name.

I study Maya, looking for signs of dissatisfaction, practically sniffing the air for her loneliness. She is clearly a kid who exists apart from other children almost every hour of almost every day of her life. And yet, despite my scouring her expression and tone for her disconnectedness, trying to angle questions in her direction that will yield some admission, some revealing detail, she simply seems to be a happy kid. She'd be a great subject for John Cacioppo's study that found that young adults who feel lonely actually spend no more time alone than those who feel more connected.

—

I can't help but wonder how Maya will feel in a year or two, when she steps through the one-way door of adolescence. For me, being the only member of a household without power was the experience of being—to steal a line from Walter Mosley—"always outnumbered, always outgunned." There was no peer in the same disadvantaged state; there was no strength in numbers.

It was in high school that I began referring to my parents as the United Front. At the time I didn't know that I was referring to a Communist strategy to join together unaffiliated workers: inclusion and coalition building was the opposite of what I meant to conjure. What I meant—and I mean it and use the term still, even in my thirties, even with a kid of my own—was that it was little me, powerless and misrepresented (when I was represented at all), against the formidable allied authority of my parents. They set my (absurdly early) curfew. They determined the best way to load a dishwasher (their way). They ruled on whether my room was clean enough (it wasn't, not by a long shot, but the force of the ruling felt draconian to my teenage sensibilities). As Nicole Campione-Barr of the University of Missouri's Family Relationships & Adolescent Development Lab comments solemnly, "Parental authority is especially inescapable for only children. Parents will always win. There's no one else to appeal to. It's that simple."

It seemed to me, from the vantage point of the messy bedroom where I spent my many grounded high school evenings behind a closed door, that with someone else to witness the arguments, or deplete the intensity of the United Front, perhaps their absolute power might not have corrupted as absolutely. This is, without exception, my biggest fear about making Dahlia an only child. I know that if any couple could be presumed to be liberal and understanding parents of a teenager, it would be my parents. And yet I know that without another kid to distract them from every curfew blown, or hateful thing said, or god knows what, they became, to my adolescent mind, tyrants. I can work to mitigate the tendencies of the United Front, but without another child in the house, she will always be as outnumbered as I was.

Numerous psychologists I've interviewed say I'm lucky that my parents were, and are, so united. (Not to mention how lucky I am that there were two of them, together.) Too often, only children end up playing the pawn in their parents' own battles. I can see why they see my struggle as good fortune and also why it was positive and appropriate for my parents to refuse to share authority with their kid. And I know, in retrospect, that handling conflict with an antiauthoritarian teenager was the toughest test their marriage ever faced and that to appear so united required quietly managing conflict that occasionally stormed between them behind their own bedroom door.

But there was a loneliness that emerged from that dynamic, an unavoidable isolation that threatens every visit, even now with Justin by my side. And I know while it has felt at times like it was my unique life sentence to face down such a United Front, there's an army of millions of us outnumbered singletons who have been outgunned. Or as Jacqueline Olds—who chuckles darkly in recognition—puts it, "The plight of the only child is to be eternally ganged up on by these giants." She adds, "It's a most acute form of loneliness." Olds and I commiserate over how it's tough not to be able to compare notes with someone in the same household, how isolating it can be to never have someone else to turn to who can tell you your feelings are valid, or even simply be a witness to conflict. And Olds believes that such a feeling of isolation can creep beyond the bounds of one's family, outside the walls of one's home. "You feel different from everyone else if you don't have a sibling to suffer the same difficulties with you."

Then again, in scores of interviews, people from evolutionary psychologists to family therapists have reminded me that siblings don't tend to suffer the same difficulties from the same parents. In families with more children, different allegiances are formed, different rules are enforced, and family crises are experienced at different developmental stages. There's no such thing as a unified family experience. Carl Pickhardt warns me that wondering if a brother or sister may have evened the score tempts me to romanticize an ideal sibling relationship. The fantasy keeps me from a different reality of what might have been, which might have been an even more acute loneliness.

John Cacioppo puts it bluntly: "Families with multiple kids often aren't functional, because siblings are always being compared, the differences are always underscored, and often in a painful way." You can be an outsider in any family structure, he reminds me, and many people are. "A source of loneliness is when you don't have a shared collective identity, and most families don't actually have shared collective identities," he points out. Intellectually, I'm reassured, but emotionally I'm left longing. A friend commented to me several years ago—and clearly it's stuck with me—that I always have to be an outsider. I had never thought of myself in this way; I flinched from her words as an accusation rather than an observation. But over the years I've returned to this statement again and again, thinking about my need to wear a motorcycle jacket rather than a varsity one, to listen to indie rock when people were listening to pop and to jazz when people were listening to indie rock, to shun team sports, to feel disdain for anyone remotely insider-y—in college, at workplaces—and to write about subcultures and unpopular beliefs. Bernice Sorenson tells me, "As only children, our experience is inherently *different*, and we become who we are because of that difference. Not everyone relates, and we don't understand why, but it's our outsider status coming home to roost." It's a melodramatic line, one that reminds me of a *Brady Bunch* episode in which Jan's line "I want to be an only child" is followed by minor-key strings—the music of impending doom. I recoil from her words much as I did from my friend's years before. I wonder if they too will take on wisdom over time.

My cousin Mike has thick brows just like my father's—we resemble my dad in different ways, and look almost nothing like each other. Our closeness began in our early teens. We were marooned at a resort in upstate New York (like *Dirty Dancing*, but off-season), celebrating my grandfather's seventy-fifth birthday over endless steam-table dinners and the requisite board games. It was during a game of Pictionary that I connected profoundly with Mike, three months my junior, then of shoulder-length metal-head curls and the oversized eyeglasses that retroactively humiliate most nerds who survived the eighties. In a matter of days we became inseparable. He spent weekend nights sleeping on my parents' living room couch and took my best friend, Sarah, to our prom. My roommate in college was his senior year girlfriend—and his eventual wife. We graduated college a week apart. He was aimless; I was living in Washington with Justin—by then, one of his dearest friends—and, lacking direction, he moved down there to be near us. For three years we lived a five-minute walk from each other.

But over time, a distance set in. He had his own brother. He wasn't, and never will be, mine. Then we had our own daughters, also just a few months apart, and we found each other again. I suppose that's the advantage of family, that ability to fall apart, and fall back together. Though, in truth, my relationship with Sarah follows the same track. We had the same high school inseparablity, followed by a similar drift apart, the same awareness that her closeness with her sister can never be replicated, and the same reconnection as adults, as mothers, speaking the same language we always have. Sarah is family to me as much as anyone who shares my genetic structure.

Only children, lacking siblings of their own, tend to build a chosen family. I have done this to a greater extreme, perhaps, than others. Several years ago a couple we were close with had recently returned to their studio apartment from a year living abroad. One snowy February day, much against her will, I persuaded the wife to join me in looking at a house with hideous asphalt siding outside but warm wood floors and winsomely aged tin ceilings inside. We fell in love with it and decided on the spot—absent husbands be damned—to do the real estate equivalent of running off to Vegas together. We applied for a mortgage. We hired a lawyer. I found myself seated at a conference table in an attorney's office with Justin and our married friends. We spent hours that day signing paperwork that would legally bind us together in ways that would possibly be more complicated to dissolve than a marriage. We moved into the duplex downstairs; they settled in upstairs. Only after we had replaced the washing machine together and planted tomatoes did I learn people call what we were doing cohousing.

The number of cohousing arrangements has grown two-thousandfold in the past decade. Cohousing found its genesis in a renewed discussion of cooperative child rearing when a Danish newspaper published an article entitled "Children Should Have One Hundred Parents," long before Hillary Clinton—mother of an only herself—wrote her book *It Takes a Village.* Inspired by the notion of making a bigger family for their only child, two American architects brought the concept to the United States in the early eighties. Psychologist Susan Newman, who has written two books on only children, tells me she believes the more singletons we choose to raise, the more common living situations like mine, codified in a mortgage broker's office, will become. "What really changes, the fewer siblings we have, is how we define family," she says. "Family becomes friends and their children. They become your support system."

Quickly, our shared home became the nerve center of a sprawling makeshift family. Every week we'd gather together for Sunday night suppers with six to twelve of our dearest friends. We'd spend every July Fourth weekend by an upstate lake together, and every New Year's in Massachusetts by the beach. Meanwhile, our friends upstairs began to grow apart. We learned, just like a real family, the pain and retribution that accompany divorce.

But the family goes on, as family does. Our dear friends, Carlene and John, always part of this circle, rented the apartment upstairs. New Year's and July Fourth and regular suppers continue, with a slightly smaller—and tighter—group and occasional new additions. The now ex-husband, Eric, still shares an office with me at the house. He and John and Justin play video games in the living room, while I cozy up under the covers, reading. Carlene comes down for a spontaneous glass of wine in her pajamas; John knocks on our door on his way home from work. Like a family, we've survived it together, and we keep going.

Still, I know there's a limit to what this chosen family can give me. I watched a decade of my mother's life ruled by the care of declining parents—a mother whose body long outlasted her mind, a father whose mind long outlasted his body. Ten years of constant and sudden flights from Boston to Florida to encounter failed surgeries and misprescribed medications, the roar of CNN at top volume providing a relentless soundtrack to confusion, depression, and worse. My mother's days between meetings and meals consisted of impossibly navigating the dual labyrinths of grief and the health care system, her midnights awaiting the shock of a ringing phone. And that's with two brothers who shared the burden. They were just as committed to their parents' care as my mother was. What will it be like for me alone?

For all the disconnection we can experience with our parents, most every only child I've interviewed or known admits a consuming dread of the loneliness we'll feel without them. This is the Greek tragedy of only childhood: our parents' death and dying. I obsess over losing them, unable to imagine myself in a world of their absence, swatting away scenes from my beloved grandparents' last years now recast with my still-vigorous parents. My anxiety of consigning Dahlia to that shared fate has begun to creep into my insomnia. A number of studies have found that eldercare tends to be mainly shouldered by one child. No matter how many siblings one might have, the nearest-residing daughter is most likely to do it all alone. Still, a 2001 study found that one of the most consistent self-perceived challenges for only children was concern about being the sole caretaker for aging parents (including feelings of anxiety about being the sole survivor in the family once their parents died). My parents address my unspoken anxiety with monthly payments into a long-term health care insurance plan. Many are not so fortunate as to be able to afford such expensive planning. And for those who are, there are still limits to what can be managed by logistics.

Justin is like a son to my parents. He will be the first to spoon pureed food into my mother's mouth, like he did for my grandmother, or help my father in the bathroom, like he did for my grandfather. And yet I know my parents are not his—he does not reside within the impossible tangle of love and authority and rebellion and pride and heartbreak that knits together parent and child. When my parents die, he'll grieve; he'll experience deep loss. But it won't have the resonance of a lifetime, of all he has ever known. And when his own parents die, he'll still be able to see in his sister's eyes the eyes of their mother. He'll have their rituals, and their memories of rituals, whether they practice them or even speak about them. It might be a divergent set of memories, scenes shot from different angles, with different emphases, maybe even different recalling dialogue, but it will be something. We onlies, we fear the nothing. We fear the winds that howl around the last one standing. We fear the black silence of carrying those ever-fading histories alone.

While that grief remains unimaginable to me, despite my chronic anguished conjuring of the nightmare to come, I can only think that to confront that loss alone is perhaps the deepest form of loneliness. John Cacioppo says he doesn't think it's a deeper crisis for singletons than it is for anyone, that divorcées (which will be half of us) and the elderly (which will be all of us, should we make it that long) experience the crisis of life alone as acutely as anyone else. In fact, researcher Norval Glenn, analyzing data from seven separate General Social Surveys, wrote in the September 3,

1984, *Journal of Family Issues* that because only children are "more emotionally self-sufficient and better able to deal with aloneness than are persons with siblings, they should be better able to cope with any social isolation that comes with old age."

And yet the lived experience can expose complexities cold data cannot reveal. I had the good fortune to meet a geriatric doctor named Jerry, who grew up without siblings on a rural Midwestern back road. His wasn't a childhood of rural isolation—nearby was a family with a mess of kids who he took on like siblings of his own. In school he made close lifelong friends. Later he married a woman he adored who was to become like a daughter to his parents. In his practice, he lovingly counsels the elderly through their last days; he not only guides their children through the medical process but helps them to manage their grief. While we talk, his pager buzzes every several minutes, warning of one possible death after another. "This is where I live every day. I think I've got a hold on it. But when my parents became ill, I knew the whole house of cards would fall," he tells me.

Indeed, when his father died—in the arms of Jerry's wife—the feeling of isolation began. Jerry's chosen family, his friends from childhood, came from all over the state for his father's funeral, overflowing the church. One friend he hadn't seen in years, a union laborer, said he had told his boss that morning, "I don't care if you fire me, I'm not missing that funeral; I'm not leaving my buddy alone." It was reassuring, and yet. Now, a year later, Jerry's mother is dying. "Now it's happening. Now I feel like the bottom is falling out," he tells me. "If I'm not qualified to handle this, who is? I'm happily married, I have a great career, wonderful friends, my church—but when they're gone, you're the only person left. And there's no getting around it." Then again, grief is grief—it may be different according to the circumstances, but it devastates everyone. There simply is no way to escape what is as inevitable in life as our own mortality, that it feels like death itself when we lose the people we love the most, whether we face that pain with or without siblings.

THREE

GOOD FOR NOTHING

t's discussed as though it's the law of the jungle, something so established in nature and common sense that it needs no defense: children without siblings are not forced to share resources, and therefore they are more selfish.

But meet Verreaux's eagles, which can be found throughout the African landscape. The elder chick pecks its sibling to death within three days of hatching. One observer counted 1,569 pecks one bird delivered to its little brother over a brutal long weekend. The Galapagos-dwelling blue-footed booby is not quite as ruthless. Older chicks limit their siblings' food intake so as to keep more for themselves and will practice siblicide only if their own body weight drops by about twenty percent. (Booby parents do not intervene in these conflicts: they practice my in-laws' theory of "feed them and stand back," only in this case there's not quite enough to feed them.) And talk about giving one's eyeteeth: these are the knife-sharp chompers that piglets are born with to defend their mother's milkiest teats from the hungry mouths of their siblings, hoarding the richest supply for themselves. Spadefoot toads are a bit more vicious. They develop lethal teeth that they use to devour their broodmates simply for the protein. That, my friends, is the law of the jungle.

Our evolutionary psychology, if not our actual behavior, is that of the spadefoot. Just ask Frank Sulloway, who compiled this information to help us understand why elder borns tend to have different characteristics from their younger siblings. All resources within a family are limited, whether those resources are Barbies or brownies. Or, more important, parental attention. Consequently, selfishness is natural between siblings, with competition sometimes exploding *Lord-of-the-Flies* style.

It's long been assumed that there are great benefits to surviving siblinghood and sharing the material and psychological offerings—or deficits—of a common home. We take this developmental advantage as a given, despite how siblings flinch when they recall enduring the awareness that one child is your mother's favorite (and it's not you), or a brother's daily torture (the BB-gun wounds my uncle inflicted upon my mother's posterior may have healed, but the psychological ones have lingered).

Infants are known to have what's known as global empathy. They cry when they hear another baby's cries; like so many tiny Bill Clintons, they can feel your pain. But around their second birthday, something called egocentric empathy develops, meaning toddlers realize that it's good for themselves to be good to others. Child psychologists call this prosocial behavior—i.e., handing over that Power Ranger because it's the nice thing to do—which begins around age two. (Not surprisingly, this is when guilt and shame also arise in the consciousness—both always stellar motivators.) Most older siblings are still only children at this age. In other words, the supposed socializing effects of a brother or sister are irrelevant.

We all function in terms of egocentric empathy. Narcissism is another thing. Perhaps W. H. Auden summed it up best when he wrote, "We are all here on earth to help others: what on earth the others are here for, I can't figure out." Narcissism is not just about seeing the world as your mirror but, rather, demonstrating a willingness to exploit others, an inflated sense of self-importance, and failing to feel empathy—egocentric or otherwise. Sigmund Freud, in his essay "On Narcissism: An Introduction," differentiated between pathological self-absorption and simply finding an interest in oneself. I like to imagine Freud watching the eighties weep-fest *Beaches,* snickering with recognition at the now-famous line, "But enough about me—what do you think of me?" Bette Midler's brassy character's faults all turn on the singleton stereotype: as she gets older, her mother packs her bags for Florida "where it's quiet" to get away from her only child's incessant demands for attention.

Dating back to the Stanley Hall days, people have voiced the belief that only children are the chief narcissists in our midst; since we don't have to share attention with our siblings, we must be dripping with self-obsession. Decade after decade, researchers dust off a common diagnostic test called the Narcissistic Personality Inventory to prove this assumption. Except the hypothesis always fails. For example, a 1989 study conducted at the University of Tennessee found, contrary to the researchers' expectations, that narcissism is not a reliable correlate of only-child status. Then in 1996 a team at Loyola College believed that there was a foundation for the assumption in what's known as "social learning theory"—we learn from one another, and if there's no "another" at home, we must not be socialized beyond ourselves—

and used the Narcissistic Personality Inventory to test their hypothesis. But this time as well, the numbers failed to show that only children were different from anyone else.

Most recently Jean Twenge, a psychologist at San Diego State University, whose books include *The Narcissism Epidemic* and *Generation Me,* did her own testing. Twenge found that about two-thirds of students she's tested have above-average scores for narcissism, which is up about eighty percent from 1980 (the year that ended the Me Decade). Yet singletons aren't overrepresented in any way. "We couldn't believe this," she tells me, "but we just couldn't find anything statistically significant." She still doesn't believe it—she's currently working on a wider sample.

Carl Pickhardt outright dismisses the idea that onlies are inherently rabid egoists. Furthermore, he says they can easily be taught to avoid the selfish trap. "The issue is because onlies get so much attention, they're really good attention getters. But you have to parent them to be good attention *givers*," he says. "You have to socialize them so that they are a part of something larger." That something larger can be as simple as going to school—there's no room in a classroom, or the playground, for outsized egocentrism. Or as Nicole Campione-Barr says, from her vantage point at the Family Relationships & Adolescent Development Lab, "It's simply not possible to get through compulsory education with the sort of selfishness people imagine only children have."

Even though I've gone cross-eyed examining charts and data sets on onlies and selfishness, even though I've studied and parsed and deconstructed the stereotype, it still creeps into my consciousness every time my daughter refuses a friend access to her trunk of spangled dance costumes: *she's a selfish only child.* I often think back to something George Hearst wrote in a letter about his only child William Randolph: "There's one thing sure about my boy Bill. I've been watching him, and I notice that when he wants cake, he wants cake; and he wants it now. And I notice that after a while he gets his cake." But Dahlia's best friend, Lucas, who at four still has no siblings, is a champion sharer. And as a dad friend remarked when I confessed to flashing on the stereotype when his sons were over for brunch recently—"My kid is a big brother, and he's just as much of an a-hole."

Pervading many singleton studies is the hypothesis that if siblings provide critical learning experiences for each other, the absence of siblings must mean that these lessons are not learned. Except that hypothesis rarely lines up with the data. John Cacioppo emphasized this when he told me that instead of operating in terms of *that's mine,* as siblings tend to do, onlies learn from mothers and fathers how to develop mature and ethical behavior in relationships. Singletons mimic how their parents share and take responsibility, rather than brawl over the remote. From parents' influence, rather than an immature sibling's, Cacioppo says, "You know you can't exploit other kids, you know you have to attend to other people, and you tend to take a greater responsibility within those relationships."

That only children are no more selfish than siblings, and often more self-possessed, rings true not just in clinical observation but in scores of data. Toni Falbo, in her cluttered office high atop the University of Texas tower, has conducted meta-analyses of more than five hundred studies over the past several decades. Combing through this mass of research and conducting a fair share of her own, she has examined sixteen traits, including leadership, maturity, extraversion, social participation, peer popularity, generosity, cooperativeness, flexibility, emotional stability, and contentment. In each and every one of these categories, only children do just as well as siblings. In only two categories has she found a marked difference between singletons and sibs: achievement motivation and self-esteem. And in those traits, onlies fared far better than kids with brothers or sisters.

Furthermore, in a large share of the studies and in ones that she has conducted herself since the meta-analysis, Falbo has found that only children are actually *more* cooperative than siblings (despite the forty-five minutes it took me to get Dahlia dressed for school this morning). Furthermore, she discovered that in her aggregation of these hundreds of studies, onlies score better in terms of their "personal adjustment." Adjustment means the ability to deal effectively with problems that are both internal, like anxiety, and external, such as conflict with others. Falbo has found that only children tend to benefit from an abundance of "parental vigilance." That attentiveness, she writes, has the tendency to "deeply influence the child's self confidence and feelings of self worth," which she says are "characteristics that figure heavily into the topic area we call personal adjustment."

To test Falbo's exhaustive findings with independent comparison techniques, psychologist Steven Mellor at Penn State sent undergraduates into middle and high school classrooms, armed with questionnaires for eleven-year-olds to nineteen-year-olds to answer. Mellor gathered the surveys, examined them for ethnic mix, socioeconomic standing, gender, and education level, and published the results in the *Journal of Genetic Psychology*. He concluded that the findings "provide much clearer support" for what Falbo has known all along. Onlies are generally more au-

tonomous, he wrote, have higher levels of aspiration and motivation, and have stronger identities, as seen in the quantitative data
on self-esteem or adjustment levels. In other words, the numbers
supported what psychologist Kenneth Terhune wrote in his 1975
book, *A Review of the Actual and Expected Consequences of Family
Size*—that only children are "more maligned than maladjusted."
But impersonal statistics—albeit impressive ones—have little to
do with how we experience the terrain of the social world.

Case in point: I'm having breakfast with my friend Donna at a
neighborhood place we frequent together every couple of weeks.
I've just dropped Dahlia off at school, and I'm a tangle of parental
anxiety, which for me is an unusual state. Dahlia has been crazy
for school since she started going at eighteen months—crazy for
her friends, crazy for her teachers, crazy for the classroom environment. But for the past few months she's railed against going
to school not just in the morning, but at bedtime. My usually
effusive and social kid has become taciturn and withdrawn. I can
hardly pause my litany of concern long enough for Donna to
order coffee. And when I do, Donna just cocks her head and peers
skeptically at me from behind her cat-eye glasses.

"What?" I ask after a long silence.

She holds my look a beat longer before she says, "Well, it's
the only-child thing, isn't it?"

"Meaning?" I ask, taken aback.

"She's an only child. So she's precocious to the point of ex-
cluding people. You know this. And it's making her left out. And
withdrawn. She doesn't have anyone on her team. It's why I was
miserable before college. And it looks like she will be too."

I'm stunned. An only child herself, Donna is social and

beloved. Furthermore, she's an academic who has conducted surveys, analyzed statistics, and written books on what she's discovered about human development. I've told her all about the findings that have mounted over the past century and I remind her of such. She just shrugs and starts talking over me.

"All I know," she says, "is that I never had a teammate. I was always left out. I was the lonely, maladjusted kid. I played with kids from the neighborhood, and they all had siblings. I went home alone. I was miserable at school every day. It's simply what happens when you're an only child."

She interrupts herself to ask a waitress for our regular orders. I take the opportunity to comment that her experience growing up wasn't the same as mine, that her Rhode Island community and Catholic school were dominated by big families and that I think the isolation of being the only singleton she knew added to her sense of isolation. As I comment that Lucas, Dahlia's dear pal, is one of several sibling-less kids in her class who is exuberantly participatory and social, Donna cuts me off.

"Listen," she says over me. "She's an only child. I know what I know. I know what it means to be smarter because of it, but also what it means to be the sensitive kid. I know how hard it is to fit in because of it. If I were to have a kid, I'd probably have an only child—I'm not faulting you for that. But I think you need to own up to what you're doing to her." I have heard this language before. I wonder if Donna's mother did too.

Our breakfasts arrive, and I change the subject. I'm unsettled, and after we part, I go back to my desk, open up a binder, and flip to my file tab on studies related to stereotyping. Here's where I find the article cited simply as "Kitzmann" in dozens of recent publications on only children. In 2002 Katherine M. Kitzmann,

Robert Cohen, and Rebecca L. Lockwood from the University of Memphis published a study in *The Journal of Social and Personal Relationships* that has been used to make Donna's point for a decade. Kitzmann and her colleagues couldn't find a difference between onlies and siblings when measuring the number of close friends and "friendship quality." But they did find that when students were asked how they felt about only children on the whole instead of individual kids in their classes, they were "less liked" by their classmates "as a group."

That finding is frequently used to demonstrate that only children are less well adjusted socially than other kids. What the study really found is evidence of a stereotype. Individual singletons are indistinguishable from anyone else, but *as a type* we piss people off. The notion of singletons carries assumptions of maladjustment, notions that fall apart when they are considered as individuals. That's the stereotype at work. Most of what the researchers learned was that there was no difference in the quality or quantity of singletons' friendships, and "no disadvantage in terms of competence in dyad or individual relationships."

I search for a 2004 study entitled "Playing Well with Others in Kindergarten: The Benefits of Siblings at Home" by an Ohio State researcher named Douglas Downey. As a father of two, he thought it was time to figure out, as he tells me, "what on earth siblings could actually be good for." Downey asked teachers to rate their kindergartners in terms of social skills: whether they got into fights, how they got along with their peers, if they were loners. He found a modest but reliable difference between singletons and kids with siblings at home and concluded that siblings act, as he told me, as "social practice partners at home," with whom kids can learn how to manage disputes. "But it's hard to take seriously one single study. And it might be the only study"—other than Kitzmann, I note—"that has anything good to say about siblings." I get his point. Out of the many hundreds of studies over the years, his findings are rare, and when taken in light of Falbo's meta-analyses (in which they were all included) they add up to very little indeed.

Evidently, Downey's comment to me had been nagging at him. After our conversation, he and a colleague published a second paper in reply to his 2004 study, extending the study beyond kindergarten into middle and high school. They examined data from the National Longitudinal Study of Adolescent Health, in which more than 13,000 kids were simply asked to name their friends. They counted the names and broke them down by family size. What they found was that only children had just as many friends as kids with siblings. To Downey, this suggested that whatever nominal difference separated onlies from siblings in kindergarten quickly worked itself out and entirely ceased to matter as kids marched on through their school years, gathering friends along the way. His conclusion was that despite his hunt for the quantifiable benefits of siblings, statistically, they were back to being, as he says, "good for nothing."

I can't help but think that Downey is overstating things for effect. Or perhaps he truly believes that the broken hearts of brotherhood aren't worth much in the end. Still, what siblings are good for, simply, is the rivalry, the opportunity to be shaped by that painful tension with them. This, some researchers and psychologists believe, is important for personal adjustment. "It's really hard to learn how to deal with the ugly stuff and to stay with it, fight back, reason, negotiate," as siblings are forced to do between themselves, says Laurie Kramer, professor of applied family studies at the University of Illinois, and the mother of an only herself. "It's learning how to live within a truly ambivalent relationship." In this regard, she says, "I still think only children may have a disadvantage, and it explains why they tend to squabble with their parents instead," as I certainly did. Kramer adds that the singleton life gives us less experience "perspective taking," as she puts it. Carl Pickhardt reminds me that while only children might dream about the companionship a brother or sister might offer, in actuality, "what you miss is the chance to be shaped by competition, comparison, and conflict." The benefit arises from the pain of sibling rivalry—from having not a protector on the playground, as Donna envisions, but a persecutor at home.

So how do I square Donna's only childhood with my own? I don't think she's simply buying the stereotype. She's too self-reflective for that, and too much of a critical thinker. Plus, it's not the only time I've heard this from people about their own pasts. Most singletons I've known as either interview subjects or friends fall into the Kitzmann-like tendency of expressing the stereotype about only children while exempting themselves from description. But there are exceptions, people who plainly admit they have conformed to type. I think of Peter, who tells me he never fit in at his school in Albany and felt he couldn't relate to anyone until he went off to college (where he related with a vengeance, losing himself in ecstatic and complicated intimacies). Or Jennifer, who says she was the "misfit to end all misfits" until she crossed the Maginot Line of puberty into the profound connections of a passionate adolescence.

Trying to understand these divergent experiences, B. G. Rosenberg, a researcher at Berkeley, published an article with Janet Hyde nearly twenty years ago in *The Journal of Genetic*

Psychology asserting the idea that three types of onlies exist. The first type Rosenberg described as "talkative, assertive, poised, and gregarious." The second is "self-indulgent, undercontrolled, thin-skinned, and self-dramatizing." The third is "dependable, productive, sympathetic, and fastidious." I was momentarily fascinated when I found these categories, the same way I can be when completing a quiz in a women's magazine on an airplane. But then I realized I fit into all three categories. And what's more, the entire world population, whether they have no siblings or a dozen, fits into these categories too. (It turns out that the sample only considered singletons—Rosenberg never compared these characteristics to siblings.) In other words, you should know I'm a Virgo. Except, as a hairstylist once told me midshampoo, because I'm an early Virgo, I'm really my rising sign, which is Sagittarius.

I don't mean to say that Donna didn't feel like an outsider as the lone only child in her neighborhood. Rather, the research suggests there's nothing inherent to an only childhood that confers that outsider status. It's just hard to be different, and it's hard to lack the thing you imagine will fix your social problems, especially when everyone gets to have that thing but you. Another friend, Alysia, raised by a single father about as far as can be from a New England Catholic school, in the gay scene of 1980s San Francisco, often ascribes her tendencies to adult maladjustment to her only childhood. She also finds those same characteristics mirrored in her husband, Jeff. "We're self-centered people who want care and nurturing," she openly admits, perhaps exaggerating a bit in the generosity of confession. "We both need to be catered to. I swing the pendulum toward me and feel so much guilt about it—and then he does the same and I resent it." But Jeff isn't an only child; he has a sister. The story he tells in attempting to attribute his traits of maladjustment is that he was adopted as a child.

We all tell ourselves different stories of why we became who we are. Many onlies, I've found, tend to attribute their negative characteristics to their lack of siblings. But the data tells us that assumption is bunk on a wide level. Assessing adult singletons, in 1999 Heidi Riggio, a psychology professor at California State University Los Angeles and Claremont Graduate University, ran a gamut of personality tests on adult onlies and siblings to measure social-emotional sensitivity, expressivity, extraversion, introversion, neuroticism, and stability. Despite her hypothesis "that growing up without siblings has a detrimental effect on social skill development," she found—*all together now*—adult singletons are no worse off than anyone else. In the Netherlands, a team of researchers examined data on marriage and learned that we're no more prone to divorce than those with siblings. (They found that we tend to prefer small families and are less satisfied with our looks, nailing me on both, despite the self-esteem findings elsewhere.) Furthermore, sociologist Norval Glenn found after crunching the results of seven surveys, that "a lack of siblings may in some ways be an aid to attaining high psychological well-being in the later years." He surmises this might be related to our higher scores in self-esteem.

I mention all these findings on the phone to Alysia one afternoon. "All these studies are quite fascinating, aren't they?" she says. "But I still feel I missed out on something. I missed out on feeling not so much that I had someone to play with, or someone to help me develop, but that I didn't have someone who could make me feel like we were a unit, made more normal by our numbers."

One hundred million is a number to redefine "normal." That's how many only children there are in China today. No wonder that's where the majority of singleton research has been focused in recent years, attempting to determine if the *Sunday Times* was correct in its June 1988 prediction of "a China in the early 21st century full of selfish and dictatorial young adults."

The Chinese counterpart to Toni Falbo, and a close colleague of hers, is Xiaotian Feng, a sociologist on the leafy campus of Nanjing University and the country's leading researcher in developing an understanding of the massive population of only children. During the early eighties, Feng entered an academic culture in China and internationally that believed that while only children were higher educational achievers than siblings, the cost of such success was very bad behavior. Since that time more than 150 studies in China have examined the selfishness and adjustment of so many Sino-singletons. What the studies have found is that the Little Emperor has no clothes.

At the apex of his field, Feng has studied every detail of only childhood. This is no joke: he surveyed kids as to whether they independently "cook their own instant noodles," to whether they exhibit greater signs of "squeamishness" (onlies score higher on both counts), to how impolite kids tend to be (it's actually siblings who win on the rudeness scale). His findings in less esoteric categories will no doubt be familiar to you by now. Writing that contrary to "people's anxiety and prejudice," teenage only children fare better socially than kids with siblings. They relate better, have a greater number of good friends, and adapt to a new school environment with greater speed and fewer issues.

"This is a negative answer to the prevalent tendency to see only children as 'uncommunicative and eccentric,' 'unsociable,' 'self-centered in all respects' and 'hard to get along with,'" Feng wrote in *Only Children: Their Families, Education, and Future.* Because singletons don't have peers at home, he believes, they step up their effort to connect with classmates. "Only children get greater compensation from social behavior—this means teenage only children learn even more, are even better tempered, and become even more competent." *This deserves attention,* his papers often seem to plead.

But there's always a Kitzmann. A research team at the Shanghai Institute found different results, which led to a paper warning that only children are likely to have issues with social development. However, these findings emerged from a very small sample with a statistical difference of .05, which when applied to a sample size like Feng's, becomes meaningless. Furthermore, they neglected to control for age, economic status, and so on. Yet despite the hundred-odd studies to the contrary, the Shanghai Institute study emerges again and again in Chinese studies. It's hard to overthrow an emperor.

When I interview sociologist Xiaohong Ma, who studies demographics and fertility at the Beijing Population Research Institute, she gestures to a framed picture of her son, her only child, and says, "He's a Little Emperor—so many Little Emperors. More than two million of them here in Beijing alone." I challenge her assessment of her own child. Isn't her sense of his so-called selfishness a generational shift related to opening markets and increased consumerism? I tell her about Bing, a woman I met in Beijing years before—when I was pregnant with Dahlia—who told me something that has become a bit of an aphorism to me: "My parents didn't grow up with McDonald's. We did. So if we want McDonald's, we are selfish, we are Little Emperors.

But really, we're finally just like everyone else." I mention Feng's extensive research. Xiaohong Ma nods and smiles through my little speech, and then says, still smiling, "But one child is more of a Little Emperor." She pours me a cup of green tea, and having offered the final word on the topic, changes the subject to talk about her recent conference paper.

FOUR

STANDING OUT FROM
THE SWELLS

One afternoon in Beijing, I take a long walk. Lost in a maze of *hutongs*, I follow an alleyway until it deposits me on a wide residential street. It's midafternoon; school's just letting out. Hundreds of students spill out of the granite and glass edifice that is Beijing #11 High School, through gates that read "Endless Learning, Endless Development." They all wear red, white, and blue tracksuits, the uniform for both girls and boys, and are laden down with book-heavy backpacks. Girls pair off and giggle; boys push one another around. Most of them are only children. Several cross the street arm in arm to buy ice cream from an elderly man's cart. Others scan their iPhones as they wait for the bus under a billboard advertising the Steve Jobs biography. The rest laugh and gossip in packs as they walk their bikes past tubs of water filled with eels for sale, past a woman sitting on the road, stitching together a pile of old shoes, toward home to make their instant noodles for supper, do their homework, and study for the exams that will determine their future and how high they can climb toward the top of the high-achieving singleton heap.

When Deng Xiaoping instituted the One Child Policy in 1979, he did so not simply with the intent of reducing the number of Chinese bodies to feed, as many assume. Deng's aim was to build a population of higher achievers who could carry a massive nation of destitute peasants into a first-world power. What it would cost to yield this transformation mattered little to a man who would famously say, "It doesn't matter if the cat is black or white so long as it catches mice." Human rights had never been a top priority in the People's Republic, and how the country intended to "keep the birth rate low to enhance the quality of the population," as he put it, was about as significant to Deng as the color of a cat.

Improbably, a nation composed mainly of only children has succeeded in lifting an impoverished agrarian economy toward the possibility of world domination in a single generation. It's hard to argue with Deng's astonishing astuteness. He understood the concept of resource dilution, and what it would mean when applied to nearly a billion people, a full two years before sociologist Judith Blake published her legendary *Demography* study that coined the term.

A professor at the UCLA School of Public Health, Blake spent much of her career investigating why only children find greater success in school and in their careers. The resource dilution model she developed to understand the almost uniform discrepancy between only children and siblings is a stunningly simple concept: each child dilutes parents' resources. Such resources can be time, money, attention—everything from money available for college to the number of words spoken directly from a parent to a child. Only children receive at least fifty percent more active care time than kids in two-child families. More kids get less. And the undiluted resources of the only-child family, Judith Blake found—and others have rediscovered—give singletons a better shot at success. Onlies tend to have higher educational and occupational achievement, whether our parents stay together or not, and whether we are from rich families or poor ones.

One study in particular, called Project Talent, is worth mentioning. It tracked 440,000 kids in 1,353 American high schools, and followed up with them when they were nearing thirty. Across the board, Project Talent found that only children performed better on cognitive tests than kids with siblings. And in tests measuring thirty-two different kinds of intelligence, onlies scored higher in twenty-five tests, and equal in four. When breaking down the data, researchers accounted for socioeconomic standing as well as whether kids were living with both parents or with single parents, and the results were the same. Furthermore, in the follow-ups only children had achieved significantly more academically and had married better-educated spouses. The data lines up neatly with what we know from the General Social Science Survey: singletons tend to score higher on intelligence tests and find greater success in school and work.

To parents, or future parents, this is great news. But Justin, for one, scoffs at the idea that a higher measure of success could be a reason to stop at one. I agree with him, mostly, but I want my kid to be happy. And if Dahlia is likely to have an easier time with her vocabulary quizzes and term papers and performance reviews, I can't help but think it might aid in her happiness.

Of course, most people don't feel like Justin does, especially when there's just one kid representing a family's legacy. Part of the singleton stereotype is that we're raised by the sorts of parents who have Harvard applications on file by preschool. (Admittedly, several longtime Harvard staffers have told me on background and "only anecdotally," there's a notably outsized number of singletons on the alumni roster.) Our matriarchs are stage mothers—or tiger mothers. I often think of hearing Toni Falbo comment during a seminar discussing her recent research in China, "American parents want their kids to be happy; Chinese parents want their kids to be successful."

In Beijing I meet Tommy, the outline of whose story—like many of his generation in China—reads like a script for a propaganda film Deng Xiaoping would have approved. He was born two years after the policy was instituted, in the northern factory town of Heilongjiang. The town was built to service the steel factory and power plant there; it's where his entire family has worked since it was built in 1959. There is no bookstore within any accessible distance; "the only books you can find there are tax books and school practice books," Tommy says. "It's a cultural desert." His mother wanted him to be the first generation in his family to go to college, but what she had in mind was a local technical college; she wanted him nearby. These were high aims for a family so poor that Tommy and his parents each owned a single outfit to wear. "Literally, I owned one shirt at a time," Tommy tells me, straightening his freshly pressed button-down and taking a sip of water with lemon.

But his parents cunningly figured out how to secure some books for him to read, despite having no meat to eat. Whatever meager resources they had, they devoted to him. His aunt and uncle did the same. Now his cousin is a pilot, and Tommy is finishing up his PhD at China's top university. "This is the story of my generation," he adds. The next day I meet Qioaxao, a young marketing executive, for coffee and tell her how remarkable I found Tommy. "That's just what it is," she says dismissively. "If I'd had a brother, this would all be impossible. If my parents could have had a second child, I wouldn't have had my books; I wouldn't have gone to my school. If I had a brother, I'd still be in my town in the provinces, farming, maybe working in the factory." She stirs her latte and pushes up the sleeves of a stylish black blazer. "Because I was the only one, I got all the resources. I got books, I got to go to college . . . that's why I'm here. That's the whole point." Judith Blake couldn't have said it better.

The One Child Policy is far simpler in name than execution. In some provinces, if a family's first child is a daughter, they are permitted to try again for a son. The measure came to pass in the hopes of reducing the continuing, horrifying practice of sex-selective infanticide—aborting female fetuses or abandoning or murdering baby girls to have a shot at a much-preferred boy. Ethnic minorities are often permitted second children. Some provinces allow singletons to have two themselves. And in some wealthy regions, like in Shanghai, the policy has relaxed to permit larger families that will make greater economic contributions. (Call it ideological communism in service of economic enterprise). But even among those with permission who are living in China's teeming cities, realities of daily life make a second child feel impossible.

You would think it's just the One Child Policy that maintains the high number of single-child families in China. But talking to parents, and studying the research, a very different story emerges.

It turns out that many people in China find the reality of second children just as impossible as anywhere else. Plus, the common belief that stopping at one kid is the only way to ensure that child's achievement in this land of fierce competition has made the policy a personal mandate, as well as a state one. Certainly, one can't discount that decades of state propaganda pitching the virtues of only children has infiltrated the culture. But when you look at the lives of Chinese citizens—what is economically feasible, what they have achieved, what their goals are for their personal futures and not just the future of the nation—there's no doubt that state logic has become sound logic, propagandistic truth has become objective truth.

"People don't want more—one is successful," Xiaohong Ma tells me when we meet at her office at the Beijing Population Research Institute. In Ma's studies of why people have only children, sixty percent of people said that the policy had nothing to do with their choice. And the forty percent who said it did ranked the policy as the last reason they stopped at one: their concerns, in order, are salary, child care, housing, career. "And across the board, they added that they stop at one to have the child be successful," Ma says. "Everyone here thinks it's the only way to make a child succeed—it's actually seen as selfish and bad parenting to have another child." Ma wishes she could have made the choice to stop at one without the pressure of legislation but says she probably would have ended up in the same place (despite the fact that she sees her own son as a Little Emperor). "Sometimes I wanted more than one, oftentimes I didn't, but I think having only one was a benefit for my family," she says, shrugging. "My son does very well on his tests."

Yanting, a young mother I meet at a packed Starbucks in Shanghai mall, illustrates the stress of considering a second child. She rushes in, harried, late, and apologetic, in a blue trench coat and heels—a meeting ran late, her mother called with an issue about her son. "It's too much," she says. I can empathize. Yanting has a degree in Chinese medicine but works in sales. Her husband is a doctor. Four years ago, after her son was born, her parents, both factory workers from the countryside, moved into her two-bedroom, 325-square-foot apartment; they sleep in her son's room. The social safety net here is still the family: grandparents care for children, children care for parents, and no one has a mind to change it. "I can't imagine having the time or money to have another child, and we're actually doing well," she tells me. "But I want to make sure my son has a graduate degree like I do. And where would we put another?"

Like Ma's Beijing survey, a study in Shanghai and surrounding areas found less than two percent of parents cite the policy as the reason they have only one child. Zhenzhen Zheng, a professor at the Institute of Population and Labor Economics of the Chinese Academy of Social Sciences, conducted the survey with demographers from Nanjing University, the Brookings Institution, and the University of North Carolina. She tells me that the study found that people said they wanted two children when the choice was theoretical, "but when they have to apply that choice to the realities of their family, they say one is enough." They cite the same concerns: the high prices of apartments and how tough it is to pay for someone to look after the kid during long work hours. "We ask them, 'How much money would be enough?'" Zhang says. "And they come up with a number that seems impossible to reach, no matter what their income, poor or rich. They've decided this is the best choice for the success of the present." She pauses thoughtfully and notes,

"It's amazing how it's become totally normative here in a single generation." Zhang says it's not just a question of how little the state does to help with child care or housing or eldercare—it's that people have learned in a single generation, through a "stunning cohorting effect," that stopping at one child allows them to be parents but also allows them the flexibility to do it on their own terms, and have a child who is better equipped to live up to ever-building expectations.

I think of Qiaoxao, the young marketing executive I met in Beijing with the wicked teenage crush on Mike Seaver, whose parents split their time between the farm and the factory, while she works in a high-rise. In many ways she represents China's stunning single-generation surge from third-world emergency to first-world superpower. She and her boyfriend talk about what fun it would be to have two children, but in reality, she knows even if she could, she never would. "All the young people I know like myself, we now want the *best* for our child, all the things we had and more we want for our children," she tells me. "And for ourselves. I want a totally different life from my parents'. I want to be a professional woman with a career—I'm afraid of being a common wife and mother. That's not what we work so hard to become."

The smaller a family is, the less education and success is correlated with social origins, or so Blake discovered in numerous studies. That's not just because one education is cheaper than two or three or four, whether education means books in a Chinese factory town or twelve years at a private school. One of the resources related to achievement that becomes diluted with each subsequent birth is the number of words spoken to a child, or so found two British psychologists, Judy Dunn and Carol Kend-rick. Furthermore, an Israeli research team learned that mothers interact with only children twice as much as last-born children. (They didn't study fathers.) Numerous studies have found that the more parents talk to a child, the higher that child's vocabu-lary level is—and the higher their IQ is as well. Singletons tend to score two or three points higher on IQ tests, which amounts to forty-five points on the SAT. This rich verbal environment is the result of living in one that is more adult and, therefore, cerebral.

But this cerebral environment is not just the result of the tendency of our most educated women to have the fewest chil-dren. Social psychologist Robert Zajonc, who codeveloped the Confluence Model, which provides the mathematical basis for understanding family size and intelligence, found that as the number of siblings goes up, the intellectual environment of the family goes down, regardless of its education level. Not only do parents speak—and read—less to their kids, but the entire family becomes more "babyish," operating at the level of its youngest member. Instead of challenging the older child, interactions are dragged backward developmentally to accommodate the younger one. Or, as Blake put it, with a literalism that threatens to rankle, the family "becomes weighted with infantile minds."

As many researchers have discussed—noticeably and repeat-edly, Toni Falbo and her colleague Denise Polit—the success of singletons can be credited most often to the special relationships we have with our parents. This is another effect of resource dilu-tion: when parents are stretched too thin to manage the plural-istic conflicts of larger households, they tend to rule by a more authoritarian form of control. Conversely, Falbo contends, the typical positive relationship between only children and their parents tends to temper pressure with encouragement, establishing "positive self-image while still reaching for higher achievement."

Like loneliness and selfishness, it's hard to objectively define achievement. Phi Beta Kappa–key holders probably aren't impressed by a "My Child Is a Student of the Month" bumper sticker unless it's on their own car. As anyone can tell you, there are big fish in little ponds—and then there are blue whales. In discussing only children and achievement, I wanted to find some figures we could all agree upon, biographical icons as much as case studies in how onlies are propelled by their family dynamic. Thus the stack of biographies by my bed about singletons who have shaped diplomatic affairs, intellectual history, the state of the art, the shape of a song: da Vinci, Gandhi, Sinatra. In their stories, and I'll share just a few, themes resonate with what I've heard in interviews and what I've gleaned from studies: a lack of resource dilution is certainly one, radiant confidence is sometimes another, and both are anchored in parental devotion, for better or for worse.

I'll begin with Iris Murdoch, not just because I venerate her, but because I thought of her when I was interviewing Qiaoxao in Beijing. Specifically, I was reminded of how her novel about siblicide, *The Green Knight*, led friend and biographer Peter Conradi to write that "she would have had to sacrifice herself to a younger brother who, being male, would seriously have embarrassed her education by taking priority." Murdoch was not a child of privilege: her father worked as a junior civil servant and borrowed money on top of his mortgage to ensure that Iris could attend "intensely high-minded" schools where she was quickly named "head girl." But the resources her parents invested in her were not merely financial. Young Iris would tag along with her father to secondhand bookshops; they'd spend evenings reading and discussing children's books, poetry, and Shakespeare.

But for some onlies, investment of parental resources extends far beyond reading together or getting in hock for tuition. One story that comes to mind is of a girl growing up on the black side of Birmingham, Alabama, in the early sixties, where Bull Connor's fire hoses were trained on her neighbors. This girl's parents knew that to succeed, she'd have to do anything twice as well as the white kids in town. Her parents were ambitious—her father was a preacher and academic administrator, her mother was a teacher—and the girl was precocious. At age three she learned to play the piano and read. Her mother kept her on a strict schedule: "She would get up, read, play the piano, eat a little something, go back to playing the piano, read a little more," says a friend about her early homeschooled years. When she finally joined a classroom, her parents bought new textbooks for the entire class because the hand-me-down books from the local white school were battered and outdated.

At age eight, a tutor with a master's degree in modern foreign languages (a true rarity in black Birmingham at the time) was hired to spend Saturdays instructing this willing student. Her success to come, recalls the tutor, "wasn't by happenstance, it was by design." Piano became competitive—she was the first black student at the college conservatory in 1964—and ice skating was layered into the schedule. While most kids were grooving their way through high school in 1970, this one was up at four thirty, at the ice rink at five o'clock, skating until seven, at classes at a nearby university at eight, nine, and ten o'clock, then practicing piano for an hour, at classes at parochial school in the afternoon, home for homework and more piano practice, and if she got done in time, back to the rink. By age nineteen she was enrolled in a master's degree program in political science. "Political science? Here's the time for fainting," her father said. "Blacks don't do political science." But she did. And she became our first black secretary of state.

One relative told Condoleezza Rice's biographer, Elisabeth Bumiller, that her parents essentially robbed her of a childhood. Rice batted the notion away, scoffing that she's glad she was raised exactly as she was, "because now I can play the piano and play with Yo-Yo Ma, and I can understand a French conversation with President Chirac." It seems that Rice overwhelmed her parents' ambition with her own. Whatever conflict she might feel about what she sacrificed for such success, or how such an upbringing shaped her personally, Rice evidently chooses not to mine in public.

Perhaps she knows that this particular path to a high perch in Washington was one previously paved by someone of far greater privilege: Franklin Delano Roosevelt's only childhood reads like a tony rundown of the Rice regime. An early childhood supervised and scheduled to the hilt: breakfast at eight o'clock, lessons until eleven, lunch, lessons until four, two hours of play, supper at six, bed at eight o'clock. The lessons, of course, were supervised by pedigreed governesses and tutors, all organized by his closely watching mother, Sara, who made sure FDR was learning to read and write in French and German as his peers were just beginning to learn English. To improve his language skills, he attended school in Germany at age nine. Roosevelt was already familiar with European travel, having sailed to the continent yearly since age three. He saw Wagner's Ring Cycle performed at Bayreuth and loved it; such was his childhood. High school was at Groton, college at Harvard.

It reads like a laughable understatement to see his mother quoted, "His father and I always expected a great deal of Franklin." But beyond such trappings of privilege, Roosevelt's biographer Jean Edward Smith takes pains to discuss the support, not just pressure, he felt from his parents, and his mother's copious devotion of time simply sitting and reading (*Robinson Crusoe* was a favorite). FDR's daughter credits his mother for giving him "the assurance he needed to prevail over adversity." Or as biographer Smith wrote, "America's confidence in FDR depended on Roosevelt's incredible confidence in himself, and that traced in large part to the comfort and security of his childhood." Roosevelt's exceptionalism didn't rise simply from a family's deep coffers, which could provide a host of tutors and transatlantic voyages, but from a childhood where the pleasures of reading and talking with parents was uncompromised by comparisons to a sibling, or sharing attention with one.

Having parents believe in you above all else produces a special relationship with oneself. Would Betty Bacall have become Lauren if it were not for her broke single mother—who couldn't scramble the cash for a $17.95 coat, she remembers—who thrilled to her Katharine Hepburn impersonations? "I was exceptional to no one but her," Bacall wrote in her memoir *By Myself,* copious paragraphs of which are devoted to her mother's single-minded devotion to her daughter. "She stood behind me all the way. If I wanted to be a dancer, and actress—that was what I would be if she could do anything about it. She would help me, encourage me, while the rest of the family thought that she was mad." And so, despite the relative frivolity of theater in a life where mother and daughter shared a three-quarter bedspring and mattress, "through her belief in me and her abounding love for me, she convinced me I could conquer the world—any part of it or all of it," Bacall writes. "She put the bit in my teeth and I ran with it." Would this girl still have ruled the silver screen if her mother's energies—not to mention income—had been further impoverished by a second child?

I loved discovering that singleton Sinatra had hosted a birthday bash for Bacall in Vegas, for which he flew only child Cole Porter out to celebrate—a fantasy convention of only children. Porter had a mother who would defend her child's talent and desires against any threat, but, unlike the Bacall family, there was no shared box spring in the Porter home. His grandfather ruled a vast empire of timber and oil, but that money came with strings attached: a life based in his hometown of Peru, Indiana, military school, and then a career in business. And when he insisted on another path, Porter was cut off. His mother had to find other ways to pay for his violin, piano, and dance lessons, and for his tuition at Worcester Academy and Yale. No wonder he composed so many songs for her.

Neither Bacall nor Porter ever discussed feeling a sense of pressure from their mothers who had risked so much for their unlikely careers in the performing arts. ("Stage mother? She wouldn't know how!" Bacall exclaimed in her book.) But still, the fact that Bacall could make good on her—and her mother's—unlikely dreams was surely significant. "That I could fulfill that promise for her meant everything to me," she wrote, "that her faith and support should not have been in vain."

But like sunshine focused through a magnifying glass, all that light can warm until it burns. There's a double edge to that special relationship between onlies and their parents. For some people it floats menacingly on the surface, every time they bring home a report card or a term paper or a girlfriend to a parent's disapproval. Sometimes it carries the financial weight of student loans and sacrifice; sometimes it takes on the filial undertones of a legacy tarnished by the only person who will carry it on. Sometimes it's simply the heartache of anything less than complete satisfaction.

My parents have always been NPR junkies, my mother especially. Once, when my mother got a new car, a friend preset every station to 90.9, Boston's public radio news station. It took her months to even notice the prank. And so when I went to work at National Public Radio headquarters in Washington—first as an intern, then as a production assistant, and so on—my parents could hardly contain their swelling pride. Every week's high point was when my name was mentioned in the credits.

After a few years, I moved on to tell my own stories, and I worried that they'd never get over my departure from NPR. They swear it's not the case; that this is just in my mind. Either way, when they seem less than thrilled by an article I write, or a book I embark upon, it truly sinks me. It's an anxiety—the anticipation of that drop in my stomach, that tightness in my throat—I carry with me far more than I should. This isn't pressure my parents have put on me—it's pressure I put on myself. Sure, I still find myself resenting them for it. Sometimes I'm as desperate to bask in their approval as I was as a teenager.

Psychologists tend to understand this pressure as the result of a lack of diversity in a family. My parents have very similar values and tastes. This isn't a bad thing—in fact, I think it is one of the main reasons why they're so happily married past their fortieth anniversary. But when your kid diverges from the choices you'd make, the expectations you maintain, and the preferences you have, it can disrupt the ecology of a family's ethic in a very particular way. It becomes another enactment of the United Front aspect of parenting an only child.

In the incubator of a small, intense family, parents expect their only child to be like themselves, whether they admit it or not. I might have appeared rebellious in high school and college in my motorcycle jacket and thigh-high boots, blaring Nine Inch Nails and spouting a warped early-nineties philosophy of Marxism and identity politics that makes me cringe today. But I graduated college with a boyfriend they adored and a collection of jazz recordings that rivaled my father's, not to mention a cubicle of my own at NPR. They've encouraged me to test myself and be open about who I am, but I've always felt the truth is, they only want me to push my self-exploration to the outer limits of what they find acceptable; I can be anyone I want to be, as long as I make choices—aesthetic, ethical, political, religious—to which they relate.

Larger families are more likely to accommodate divergent trajectories and opinions. You can have jocks and nerds, skaters and goths, Democrats and Republicans, all hanging out in one parking lot after school, so to speak, in this case the dinner table or minivan. Consequently, a greater tolerance emerges. When it's just the three of you—or in some cases, the two of you—a certain intolerance emerges. You might be entirely with the program (say, like Condi was) or not, but you're sure to internalize it either way. Plus, you are the sole recipient of the parental gaze, which, as we all know, can be a withering one. "Only children are scrutinized all the time," says Carl Pickhardt, discussing how the question of pressure to achieve manifests itself in sessions in his office, leading patients to reach for the Kleenex box on his coffee table. "What makes it hard is the pressure parents feel because it's their first and last chance to do it right," he tells me. "That conveys to the child, who then carries it forward."

Just imagine how Pickhardt's observations resonate in cultures where the family name is worth everything. Namely, cultures where, to repeat Falbo's wisdom, a child's success, rather than happiness, is what governs parenting. What researchers have found studying Chinese singletons is that it's not pressure from their parents they feel so much as pressure from themselves. Xiaotian Feng at Nanjing University discovered that singletons are twenty percent harder on themselves about school scores than their parents are, when comparing statistics scoring kids' expectations for themselves versus their parents' expectations. But he's learned as well that more parents of only children hope their kids will earn advanced degrees than parents of siblings, and that only children have such plans for themselves. As Tommy in Beijing says, "My whole family loves me for my scores." But he quickly adds, "All the pressure was really from me. My parents wanted me to go far, but not this far—they're proud, but not pressuring."

Despite this pressure, Falbo has found that only children in China report less psychological distress than their peers with siblings, and high self-concept both academically and physically. The analysis Falbo and many other researchers have offered is that the parents of only children are more responsive to their needs as well as more supportive. This falls into place with the "special relationship" that enhances achievement, that we find with singletons around the world. Feng, however, found that unlike American kids, urban Chinese kids—ninety percent of whom are onlies—tend to be more neurotic, reported "higher perceived stressors," and show tendencies toward "social depression." "Of course, they study all the time, and their lives are based on their exam scores," one Chinese professor told me. "What do you expect?" Xiaogang Wu, a professor of social science at the Hong Kong University of Science, put it this way: "They shoulder the raised expectations of a single generation—here too." It's true: in thirty-odd years this region of the world has transformed into a place where luxury malls line cities, universities are overenrolled to bursting, and everyone expects to claw their way to the summit of an overpopulated mountain. "And if they can't, it's suicide," he says. I think he's being euphemistic.

Like so many of my subjects in Asia, Wu has asked me to meet him at a Costa Coffee in a glass and marble luxury mall, all gleaming escalators and display cases. We sit sipping cappuccinos, overlooking an atrium ringed with windows from the likes of Louis Vuitton and Marc Jacobs. He gestures out to the floor seven stories below us and says, "You know about the suicide, don't you?" I don't. He tells me the story. Two parents had an explosive argument about whether their newborn baby would be able to attend private school in a few years. The father said there was no way the family could afford it; their apartment was too costly, his salary was too low. The wife screamed and begged, fighting his verdict with every argument and tactic she could invoke. He ended the conversation. She said that if she couldn't put her only child in private school, she had already lost—she could imagine the child's entire future unfurling out as a tragedy of failure, and she found it unbearable. The mother took her baby to the mall, rode the escalators to the top, and flung herself, with the baby in her arms, to the marble floor below. The baby survived. She did not. "People here are willing to sacrifice anything for their children," Wu says as a coda to this narrative perversion of his statement. "And with that comes a crazy kind of pressure for everyone involved."

Should I have told that story? It was simply so jarring to sit in that interview, staring down at the marble floor so far below. It's the most extreme episode I've heard of in the most extremely pressured culture I've encountered. While all this attention can yield statistically irrefutable positive outcomes, it certainly sharpens its own edges. But I think that parents are only part of the story for most of us. In my experience, and from what I've learned through both interviews and biographical accounts, a major component of our achievement resides in our relationships with ourselves. It springs from our solitude.

As a kid, I read compulsively. I knew the word "epitaph" by age five because my parents told me mine would be, "She just wanted to finish the page." I still disappear in the morning only to emerge before dinner with a book begun and completed. There's a lot that I miss since becoming a parent—long, meandering walks getting lost in my own head, spontaneous shows and drinks and movies, staying up all night talking with friends—but most of all I miss the freedom to frequently disappear between the covers of a book. It is the activity that has probably given me the deepest— and certainly the most reliable—pleasure I have known.

I love this passage from fellow only child Jean-Paul Sartre's autobiography *The Words:* "I began my life as I shall no doubt end it: amidst books . . . I never tilled the soil or hunted for nests. I didn't gather herbs or throw stones at birds. But books were my birds and nests, my household pets, my barn and my countryside. The library was the world caught in a mirror." Plenty of people with siblings share my sentiments. But I've heard it repeated in conversation with only children (no matter what career they end up pursuing) too many times to count. In *The Solitary Volcano*—and doesn't that title say it all?—Ezra Pound biographer John Tytell wrote that more than anything, it was Pound's solitude that "freed him for his own concerns, and he had seriously tried to master all there is to know about the history and art of poetry." Even at age six, Pound was known as the Professor, for his glasses, obsessive reading, and verbosity. "He was all books," a neighbor recalled of the young boy. "Lose all companions," Pound wrote ecstatically.

Lillian Hellman was less high-minded but just as voracious as a girl, reading, as she wrote, "a dreadful magazine called *Snappy Stories* which I borrowed from the elevator man, straight through Balzac" and *Love Confessions,* which she lifted off the janitor, to Flaubert's complete works. "Books saved her from both loneliness and the company of those she could not abide," wrote biographer Deborah Martinson of Hellman reading under a fig tree in New Orleans, or curled up in the "genteel poverty" of her Manhattan apartment. Hellman couldn't care less about her academic record. Impatient with school, her bookishness was devoted solely to reading's own rapture.

Thankfully, the pop cultural stereotype foisted upon us on-screen finds its refutation on the page. True story: I'm on a doctor's table with my pregnant belly lubed up for a sonogram. Justin and I are about to learn the sex of our possible only child. All my friends had guessed it would be a boy; all the Puerto Rican ladies on the subway disagreed. When the technician doing the sonogram announced, "It's a girl!" the following sentence leaps from my mouth involuntarily: "I have the curriculum for that!"

Girls, studies show, develop extra pluck without siblings. (One of my favorite lines about Hellman is "Ten minutes with Lillian and Joan of Arc would have recanted.") Not only has children's literature been effusive about the only child, it has often focused on the female variety. Writers recognized this confidence early. Just think of the canon of great children's books, of the girls who joined me by flashlight after my parents thought I was asleep: *Heidi* (author Johanna Spyri was the mother of an only herself), Harriet the Spy, Pippi Longstocking, and my hero, for now and forever, dear, dear Anne of Green Gables. I communed with these fictional girls so many times that the pages of my paperbacks were as thin as Anne's muslin dress.

Singletons of both sexes, familiar with the richness of solitude, report far deeper interest in white collar, scientific, and cerebral career paths. "The findings are remarkably uniform," wrote John G. Claudy at the American Institutes for Research, who analyzed the Project Talent data. This lines up with similar numbers from China, showing that "many more only children expect to be in 'knowledge-type' occupations" than siblings; twice as many siblings follow careers in the military or police force than only children. Furthermore, Project Talent found that only children in high school prefer activities that are intellectual and artistic and that rely on solitude—like reading, music, and photography. Siblings tend toward team sports.

James Gleick wrote of Isaac Newton, "solitude was the essential part of his genius," and despite his abandonment by his parents and near total isolation as a boy, Einstein said of him, "fortunate Newton, happy childhood of science!" so engrossed was he in making deliberate sense of every detail of his physical world. The son of an illiterate farmer, he would spend his time making lists—of calendar days, remedies; he cataloged 2,400 nouns by subject—before he set about redefining mathematics. Charles Lindbergh was hardly a genius on Newton's level, having flunked out of the University of Wisconsin in his sophomore year, failing mathematics, chemistry, and English. But he shared this compulsive habit of list making, and, like Newton, was an obsessive collector and cataloger, amassing stones, arrowheads, coins, and stamps. But it was outside, in the wilderness, alone, where he most liked to be, where he, as biographer A. Scott Berg wrote, "developed what would be a lifelong practice of internal conversations, a series of questions he would pose to himself."

In studies that focus on birth order rather than an absence of siblings, only children and firstborns are almost always lumped into a single group. Historically, the outsized success of firstborns has been understood as the result of teaching their younger siblings—what's known as a tutoring effect. But increasingly researchers have contended that the oldest-child advantage can be traced to their first years spent without siblings, living in a family with undiluted parental investment and verbal engagement. Most recently, Steven Mellor at Penn State retested the tutoring hypothesis among eleven- to nineteen-year-olds, employing a range of independent comparison techniques. Across ethnicity, socioeconomics, gender, and education level, Mellor found that in each case, the explanation for higher cognitive scores, stronger self-confidence, more formidable academic accomplishment, and deeper ambition "favors the importance of the parent-child relationship" over what older sibs gain from teaching their younger sibs.

But despite the similar rankings—the disproportionate numbers of onlies and firstborns in *Who's Who*, among Nobel Laureates, and so on—there tends to be a significant difference between the two. Frank Sulloway's book *Born to Rebel* traces why youngest siblings are responsible for radical innovation in history, while oldest ones tend to carry on the faith of their fathers. Firstborns generally hew to their parents' beliefs and standards, which explains why they often end up in management positions; a company line often runs through their success stories. This explains why they tend to be more conservative thinkers—and voters— and are less likely to make strides to reinvent the world, creatively or intellectually.

I wondered, reading his book, if I'm simply reproducing my parents' choices in this oldest-born mold. If my own politics and predilections—including my thinking about family size—are simply a conservative echo of my mother's youngest-born tendencies. Not necessarily, he tells me. "This is the biggest difference between firstborns and only children—you are a wild card," he says. "You aren't influenced by the sibling order that shapes other people. You're freer to be influenced by other forces. You're freer to end up being who you want to be." I have no doubt Murdoch and Hellman would agree, and agree profoundly. (Feng, in China, found as well that even successful siblings, when compared to only children, seem to "have no definite views of their own.")

With that freedom, I believe, comes a more open and flexible notion of achievement. William Randolph Hearst horrified his family by dropping out of Harvard, only to become the world's first media mogul (Lincoln Steffens wrote of Hearst, "his very ability seems to be that of will rather than of mind"). John Lennon failed his O Levels—despite the fact that, like Hellman, he was reading Balzac as a child—and went on to bigger-than-Jesus status, challenged only by singleton Elvis. The one thing that appears with near-complete ubiquity in the stories of exceedingly successful singletons is, as Cole Porter once said in talking about his days at Yale, "the desire to stand out" in a class hardly lacking in "swells."

Only children tend to develop unusually multifaceted notions of themselves. Bill Bradley's trip to England as a young basketball player inspired him to become a Rhodes scholar and opened up the flexibility to succeed both on Madison Square Garden's court and later on the Senate floor. Brian May's second act after touring the world with Queen, revolutionizing guitar technique on an instrument he built alongside his father (and harmonizing "Under Pressure" with the passion that only comes from experience), was to become an astrophysicist. Hedy Lamarr was the shining star of MGM's golden age until she abandoned Hollywood to develop a secret communication system adopted by the US Navy, laying the foundation for Bluetooth and WiFi technology. "You claim more parts of yourself," Sulloway tells me, because we aren't habitually defining ourselves against a sibling. So many singletons aspire from childhood to transcend traditional ideas of success. Sartre expresses this impulse in *The Words*, when he recalls thinking, as a boy, "It is not enough for my character to be good; it must also be prophetic." His words ring with the pressure of extraordinary goals, vibrating with the freedom to become fully, implausibly, and brilliantly himself.

FIVE

WHERE SOMEONE LOVES
YOU BEST OF ALL

y grandfather Sam used to tell me a joke: There's a mother dropping her son off at the bus that will take him to overnight camp. She weeps, clenching him to her chest pleading, "Don't go! I'll miss you! I can't stand it!" Finally he relents and says, "Okay, Mom—I won't go, not if it hurts you so." She stands back and growls at him, *Get on that bus.* In my family, and in most of the single-child families I've interviewed, we are egregiously inept at *get on that bus.* Even after a lousy, tension-filled visit, even when we know we'll soon be together again (and sometimes ambivalently so), we weep saying good-bye, wrenching ourselves apart from each other, repeating my grandfather's punch line through tight, bittersweet laughter, *"Get on that bus."*

I heard my grandfather's punch line in my head while I was recently watching a documentary called *The Kids Grow Up.* It's the story of a father and a girl, who is introduced in a pink tutu, her lithe, seven-year-old form ecstatically twirling for the camera. "This budding ballerina is my daughter and only child," the film-maker Doug Block narrates in voice-over. The movie considers what it means to let go of his daughter and only child in the year before she leaves her family's apartment in downtown Manhattan to cross the country for a dorm room at Pomona College. As Lucy, matured into a stunning seventeen-year-old—a young Dora Maar in a Block Island T-shirt—says directly into the camera, "It's harder for you than it is for me and it shouldn't be."

The film stitches together footage Block shot over Lucy's entire childhood and adolescence, interviews he did regularly with her saucer eyes and aquiline nose filling the frame. For the first ten-odd years, the comfort and intimacy between the two of them is undeniable. But gradually she begins to turn away from the lens, she recoils from his questions, she meets the intensity of his electronic gaze with resentment and embarrassment. The viewer does too, yearning for him to put down the damn camcorder and give her the space to evolve without his intrusive witnessing. When I watched this film, I sobbed. Like I sobbed during *Terms of Endearment* (another heartbreaking film about an only child with an intense parent). I sobbed as a daughter; I sobbed as a mother. But this was no hospital bed tragedy, just an insightful exploration of what it means to have your kid go off to college.

There are hundreds of millions of only children in this world, all of us different. And there are almost twice as many parents of only children, also living lives entirely unique to their circumstances and personas. But there is one thing I would put my money on us all having in common, in every single-child family around the world: the emotional lives of our families are amplified. The gaze is more intense, the love undiluted (to borrow from Judith Blake). And the conflict is fierce. This amplification is the longest, sharpest edge of the double-bladed sword that is only childhood. It's not the loneliness, or selfishness, or maladjustment that we worry about. It's the amplification, the intensity. It's the reason some adult only children have told me they were entirely committed to making sure their first child had a sibling, and the reason others have told me they'd never have more than one kid.

We were on a nightly tear through *Where the Wild Things Are*, sometimes reading it three times in a row. When Max tired of the rumpus, yearning to be "where someone loved him best of all," Dahlia would burrow into me. I'd finish the book, draw up her quilt (which she'd instantly kick off), give her a kiss, and whisper in her ear, "I love you best of all." Every night for months I murmured the same words before I switched off the light. I never mentioned to Justin how I would say good night to Dahlia. I liked having a secret ritual with her. But one night, when I leaned down to whisper the words in her soft pink ear, it hit me: in a home of siblings, no parent would ever say a child was loved best of all.

So I stopped. For a while at least. Then I realized my mindfulness was enough. I didn't need to summarily issue the blackout of an expression, though perhaps codifying my sentiment as ritual wasn't the best idea. Then I began to say it occasionally, aware of the complexities of both the reality of my undiluted love and how I express it. And one quiet winter afternoon, over mismatched mugs of steaming coffee in the kitchen, I use Maurice Sendak's words as a way to begin a conversation about this love with Justin, who never knew being loved best of all himself, and has seen both the wonders and madness that such love has conferred upon my own childhood and the adulthood it produced.

"This is one of the most special things about having an only child," he says. "You can eat her up every day without having to think that much about expressing these things fairly to each child." I nod, thinking about the myriad studies I've read about how every parent admits to having a favorite, and how parents and kids often pair off one favorite to a parent, creating familial divisions. Then my mind wanders back to his words "eating her up," thinking about how I literally do feel like I can consume her, devouring the perfect curves of what I call her "brioche butt" as she giggles with abandon. I know the days of this deeply physical intimacy with her are waning. Someday soon my affection will embarrass her; someday soon we'll take our last giddy bath together. I'd say that someday soon we'll no longer cuddle in bed and talk, but I know better—in my late thirties I still do this with my parents, and I've found my confession of this fact reciprocated in conversation with many other onlies (though women all).

"It's not so complicated at her age," Justin continues. "There's a certain purity to loving a four-year-old. But you and I both have to prepare for the fact that the intensity of our love will become complicated for her." He gets up to pour some more coffee, smiling at me sweetly, sympathetically. "I often get the sense of you wanting to absorb her. You have this feeling—and I really do relate to it—that you can't get quite enough. But I know you know how that turns out. We need to accept that eventually that isn't going to be reciprocated. That's the trick, I think, of having an only child. I know it's a cliché—Jesus, it's a Sting song—but you gotta set her free. And it's messy for everyone." No wonder I tear up whenever I think of Lucy Block turning away from the camera. No wonder I feel her exasperation as deeply as her father's loss.

That night Dahlia is testy with me at bedtime. As I tuck her in, I tell her I love her. She huffs and turns away from me. I read her a book. I kiss the back of her head and say, "I know you love me, baby." "No," she says in her most clipped, dismissive voice. I read her another book. By the end of it, she has rolled over and curled into my arm. She looks up at me with wide hazel eyes and says slowly and solemnly, "I do love you, Mama." She angles up for a kiss. The arc is complete. This arc is mildly wounding when stretched over twenty minutes with a four-year-old. I know in the future this arc will break my heart when it is stretched over hours, then days, and possibly even years.

Dahlia won't always insist on singing along to Johnny Cash or dancing like a little maniac to the Pixies. More important, she'll develop her own definitions of who she is and wants to become—not to mention who she thinks we are. Her life will change and her expectations of life will change. If she remains our only kid, we won't have other evolving young lives in our household to compare hers to, other recalcitrant behaviors or objectionable tastes, or emerging belief systems, or modes of communication. My own evolution entailed wearing reconstructed vintage clothing and slamming my door hard enough to shake our whole apartment; it meant parents who went rigid with horror during my dark tunnel of adolescence. And for all of us, it left scars.

But still, when it's just the three of us, me and my parents, sharing a bottle of wine, when Justin is away on assignment and Dahlia has gone to sleep, that's my platonic ideal of family happiness, right there. Justin has been long embraced into our team. But when the three of us are alone—or with Dahlia—and my mother and I aren't overreacting to each other's every word, it can be the most complete form of contentment I know, rivaling when Justin,

Dahlia, and I gather in a tangled threesome for "family hug," as my kid calls it. Four decades of intensity are a lot to compete with.

I know that Dahlia may end up finding herself at a distance from Justin and me in her political, religious, and aesthetic preferences. But I hope she'll still be able to wind into my arm and say, "I do love you, Mama," at the end of the day. Whether she can is riding less on her, I believe, than on whether we can give her the room—without the judgment—for that profound reflection and experimentation.

It all comes back to the notion of the single-child family as a fascist state. It's an inherent aspect to being the lone citizen under the jurisdiction of the United Front; the unavoidable outcome of being always outnumbered, always outgunned. But different families manage it in different ways. Condoleezza Rice's parents encouraged her to choose what they would all eat for dinner, how they would all dress in the morning, what they would do with the occasional hours she'd step away from the piano or her textbooks and spend time as a threesome. The Rices went as far as electing her "president" of the family. "I won it fair and square," she told an interviewer. "My mother and I voted for me." And yet when young Condi and her friends wanted to perform a Supremes number in a talent show, the president was vetoed: considering her choice unseemly, her parents hired a tap dance instructor and ordered a costume for her so she could take the stage in a manner they deemed appropriate for their daughter. (Her biographer writes that Mr. Rice, with the commanding presence of a preacher, stood by the stage with his arms crossed to make sure no one laughed at her.)

Families manage authority and individuation across quite a spectrum, often depending on how the relationship between parents functions. A team of researchers at Seton Hall observed in an article in *Psychological Reports* that the single child family often functions excessively as an "individual, indivisible unit," without the individuation necessary to foster one's own selfhood. Carole Ryan, a singleton herself, whose research and own counseling practice focused on the experience of only children, published a paper in *The Family Journal* on related strategies for professionals, who, on the whole, had devoted "minimal counseling attention to this specialized family system," she wrote. One of her main suggestions for psychologists was to identify the characteristics of how boundaries are drawn in the single-child family, using the work of an Argentinean therapist named Salvador Minuchin, whose writing in the 1970s significantly influenced the practice of family therapy. Minuchin found that boundaries tend to fall into three categories: "clear," allowing for each member's self-defined individuality; "rigid," meaning inflexible, pushing family members outside the unit to develop their own support system; and "diffuse," or the opposite of rigid, meaning overly enmeshed and preventing family members from developing their own autonomy and individuality. You can imagine how in the intense, parent-majority triangle of the single-child family, these categories would radically define how a kid could develop.

The categories go a long way toward making sense of the broad spectrum of singleton stories. It explains, in part, how FDR stuck happily with his parents' program, and how William Randolph Hearst cast himself as a rich-boy renegade. It explains why an Australian singleton tells me that he "had to make a family outside my family, because all they ever did was judge," while an adult only child from Florida admits, "I just thought they gave me everything, including who I am—I never understood rebellion." And yet, I feel like my own family swings between all three categories, with equal intensity, in ways that have defined me, and our threesome, with equal force.

Families are constellations in three dimensions, not simple points on a plane. In households of two parents and one child, the relationship between parents determines the culture of that household, and the child needs to figure out what role to play in that relationship. I'll call it "marriage" for shorthand, but I mean any cohabitating parents, legally tethered or not. Minuchin gets credit for developing the categories I'm about to lay out, but it was a team of academics across disciplines—linguistics, adolescent psychology, educational psychology—at the University of Texas who researched how being raised in the shadow of different types of marriages can shape the only child. What they found is that it all simmers down to how much a child is cast in a mediator role in the parents' relationship. Everyone is shaped by his or her parents' marriage. But for those of us who are the only members of what's known as the sibling subsystem in a family, the effects are intensified.

The marriage I know best is the "individuated" one, which allows for both autonomy and connectedness. It permits a kid to see parents as individuals who work out their own conflicts, setting a culture at home for healthy individuation and allowing an adolescent, as Minuchin wrote, to "leave home," both literally and figuratively. I believe I was lucky to be raised in the context of such a marriage, and that I'm equally lucky to have built one of my own. Which is not to say that we're immune to conflict. But while I was embroiled in my own issues growing up, I was never called up to the bench to participate in theirs. And my parents' comfort with their own relative differences was instructive to me.

They had no need to get lost in each other, nor to disappear from each other. And yet, to be a third wheel to a happy marriage is a strange role to fill. As a kid, when my parents would hug and kiss, I would wedge my small body between theirs. We'd all laugh. It was a running joke, but I made my point. Dahlia gets similarly impatient when Justin and I exclude her from our intimacy.

If my parents, or Justin and I, were more apt to practice the art of We Two Become One, Minuchin would consider such a marriage "enmeshed." That's when parents tend to agree on everything, share a conjoined identity, and offer their child little freedom to develop a unique worldview. This is the United Front at its most extreme. And if I railed against what felt like family fascism in my own home, I can only imagine a life governed by an even more self-aligning marriage. (To be honest, I found very, very few singletons who appeared to have been raised in such a family. The ones I spoke to were often second- or third-generation only children, raised by socially progressive parents, who seemed devoted to encouraging their kid's individuality—which resulted in their own values and cultural preferences updated to a more pierced and post-punk generation.)

Its opposite is the "disengaged marriage"; basically, when parents are disconnected from each other but become so apathetic about the relationship that they don't bother to have any outward conflict about their differences. Kids are exposed neither to arguments nor to their resolution and tend to withdraw from their families. This can yield an apathy that mirrors their parents', or it can grant the freedom singletons often fail to find in other family dynamics, letting them fully define themselves on their own terms. But growing up under a disengaged marriage is by no means simple. Often parents try to cast their child as their primary relationship in the family, lacking intimacy with a spouse. "My dad would try to get me to be 'his,' so to speak," one man who was raised without siblings in such a household in suburban Albany tells me. "But when I was twelve or thirteen, I got closer to my mother. He wanted me to play sports, and I couldn't care less—I just wanted to go to the movies with my mom. It was a nightmare. I was caught in the middle; they were barely talking. So I just shut down. And then in college I completely rebelled— but it's not like I knew who I was before I left the house, and it's not like I ever learned how to fight," he says, studying his hands, suddenly becoming silent.

The more explosive version of his parents' relationship is the "conflictual marriage," marked by little connectedness between two highly individual parents. Like disengaged marriages, con- flictual ones are especially tough on only children, as we tend to be "triangulated," as psychologist Carole Ryan puts it, and turn into mediators. In *The Drama of the Gifted Child*, the semi- nal book about how parents screw up talented kids, author Alice Miller discussed how kids in these triangles develop the ability to meet others' needs, but fail to take care of their own, as they are called upon to provide the unqualified love and acceptance their parents crave but fail to receive in such relationships. And when one parent feels the dissatisfaction of his or her marriage more acutely, there exists a tendency to pull a child into his or her own crisis, as both a teammate and life raft. The pain of this role is exactly why one mother of three was hell-bent against having just one child. "That level of emotional responsibility for my mother is something that I've always dealt with. The lack of appropriate boundaries, the excessive emotional enmeshment—it had a hor- rible effect on me, and I knew plenty of only children growing up who were in similar positions, and who it had a horrible effect on too," Ryan tells me. "I'm never putting my kids in that position, where my own unhappiness is their responsibility. I know that's not everyone's story—I know it's not yours. But for me, it had a lot to do with being an only child. And I never, ever, would want my kids to go through that."

Of course, more than half of American marriages end in divorce. And for only children, the chances of growing up in a household with both of one's parents are even slimmer. There are myriad reasons why parents intentionally opt to have only one kid. But not wanting to bring another child into a crumbling marriage, or simply not having a partner with whom to raise a second or third kid—these are circumstances that often limit family size. Many singletons remain such because their parents split up before they have another child, so there tends to be a disproportionate number of us in single-parent families. Parents frequently go on to remarry, and in their later marriage will often have more kids, but life as an only child during the dissolution of a marriage, and living with no-longer-coupled parents, is an exercise in survival, often pushing the bounds of intensity.

Amanda has no memory of her parents together in the same room. When she was two, living in a Denver suburb, her dad had come home one day and announced that he didn't like being a husband or a father, and left. Her mother had planned to go to college, but instead had moved to Colorado to marry him. Now she had nothing but a high school diploma and a daughter, far from the Iowa town where she'd grown up. She remarried a few years later. Amanda's stepfather was chronically depressed, verbally abusive to everyone, and couldn't hold down a job. Her mother would get up at four to roll newspapers, then make a hot breakfast for her husband, then head off to the dermatologist's office where she worked the front desk. She spent evenings at Amanda's basketball games before coming home in time to make dinner. After her stepfather's son died from a drug overdose, the brittle marriage couldn't bend to accommodate the fallout from such a stunning tragedy. When her stepfather left her mother, Amanda says she knew more than ever, "I had to be her life. She didn't have anybody. I mean nobody at all. Nobody but me," Amanda says. "Honestly, I am still her life. Almost thirty years later, I'm still her whole life."

Compulsively smoothing her halo of red hair, Amanda tells me she can't recall a single day of her childhood that wasn't consumed with anxiety for her mother. "I spent most of my life trying to do whatever I believed would make her feel content or calm. I didn't want to cause more friction. *I* had to look out for *her*—from the time I could remember anything, I knew I literally was responsible for her." But Amanda's mother insisted she go off to college—she didn't want her to suffer a similar fate. "My mom moved my stuff into the dorm that first day, went down into the parking lot, and just cried and cried and cried," she remembers. "I couldn't stop crying because I didn't know if she was going to be okay, but I had to hide that from her, why I was crying. So many moments like that, I had to hide from my mom. And it didn't stop there. Through my whole adulthood I've known that the only way she can do anything is through me." Before she got married, Amanda made sure her husband understood, "It's a package deal, me and my mother. Marrying you isn't going to change the fact that I'm all she has, and that she'll always mean everything to me."

On New Year's Eve of last year, Amanda's mother was diagnosed with cancer. She was told she might live for twelve months
with the help of chemotherapy. "I was there at that appointment.
And I was such a mess that after a certain point all I can remember is the oncologist saying, 'Go get the social worker.'" And
Amanda has been at every appointment since; there's no one else
to take her mother to chemo every day. Even now that Amanda
has three kids of her own, her life is still primarily dedicated to
caring for her mother. She feels profound guilt about the time
and energy it takes away from her own kids, time and energy
she feels her mother would have never taken away from her. And
she worries that both the emotional and temporal intensity of
her commitment to her mother will never wane, even after she's
died. Amanda takes off her copper-rimmed glasses and wipes her
eyes. "I don't know how to even imagine getting back to a normal
life—all my life is, is this urgency. I cry all the time. And I know
I'm going to be sad every day for the rest of my life."

I find Amanda's story unusually heartbreaking, but elements
of her struggle are actually not that unusual at all. It's hardly uncommon for only children to care for their parents when a family finds itself shattered, just when they most need parents to be
caring for them. As psychiatrist Margaret Schilbuk wrote in an
article in the *American Journal of Orthopsychiatry*, parents sometimes "abdicate the parental role," or use their child as a partner in
working through their own "discordant parental symbiosis"—and
this often happens, she writes, when they have just one child.
This is the case particularly "when a mother alone represented
a parental subsystem," and it's the worst if a mother still fancies
herself a teenager when her kid reaches adolescence, she says,
drawing from the experience of her own practice. It's one thing

not to reach psychological autonomy, but many only children from divorced families have told me about ballasting their mother's quotidian autonomy as well. No doubt this happens with fathers too, but the stories I've heard have, with only one exception, been about mothers.

Two adult only children I met recounted teaching their mothers to drive after their fathers had left. "It was genuinely traumatic, bizarre, to be mothering my own mother like this at age seventeen," one of them tells me. "I'm never going to teach anyone to drive again—not even my kids. It's the moment when I realized how dysfunctionally intense everything had become. I still think about it more often than I'd like, twenty years later." Many others have told me about assuming the role of a spouse when their three-person family dropped down to two; this is particularly the case with sons recast as husbands in the aftermath of a separation. "Still to this day" (twenty years later) "my mom won't date," one single-mothered singleton says. "I don't know if it's because she had me to dress up and go out to fancy restaurants, just the two of us. It was like date night every week, but with my mom and her little kid. I'd order the crab legs." This phenomenon of the child-date is inherently specific to a single-child, single-parent dynamic.

An article by a team of psychologists in *The Journal of Child Psychology and Psychiatry* presented data that supports what most of us already assume, that a positive sibling relationship is a protective shield against marital conflict and dissolution. And, movingly, the powerful "effect of sibling affection" was found, in family crisis, to override the effect of even the mother-child relationship. Just as that's a significant bond to hold on to, it's an equally significant bond to lack in such circumstances. As Carl

Pickhardt tells me, divorce tends to be even tougher on only children because singletons are more consistently "sensitive to the pain of their parents, which makes it infinitely harder." Siblings who have survived divorce together often say they'd never stop at one child, fearing they'd deprive their kid of a teammate when things fell apart. And most of the singletons I've talked to who've endured it alone tend to consider it nothing short of prolonged trauma. As one woman, whose only childhood was spent shuttling back and forth over state lines as a pawn in her parents' unending conflict, puts it in particularly bitter terms, "Sentencing me to go through that without a sister or brother was nothing short of child abuse."

And yet a study by Denise Polit complicates that narrative. In intensive, open-ended interviews with more than one hundred divorced mothers with different numbers of children, Polit tested the assumption that divorce is tougher on onlies. What she learned is that such "sentencing" might actually have been a blessing. First, the quantitative: Polit found, by the numbers, that only children actually seemed to have an easier time coping with the pain of divorce. Based on their mothers' accounts, thirty-five percent of children in two-child families would continue to manifest signs of anger or distress about the divorce in its aftermath, whereas only four percent of only children did. Children in two-child families were significantly more likely than only children to have a hard time beginning and maintaining friendships, to be overly shy with both kids and grown-ups, and to prefer being alone to being social in the aftermath of a separation. Mothers of siblings rarely said that they had actually helped each other through the emotional terrain of the post-divorce period. "Sibling rivalry and competition for the mother's attention after the divorce often undermined the potential for mutual support," she found, contrary to popular belief, and "exacerbated feelings of insecurity stemming from the father's departure." Plus, the only children in these studies rated as more highly autonomous, mature, and empathic for their ages.

But there's a qualitative side to the study too: not only did Polit run surveys, she interviewed respondents as well. The interviews with mothers of onlies, she writes, "were permeated with a sense of their strength, self-confidence, and optimism," and were the "most introspective, planful, and in touch with their needs of any of the women interviewed." They typically were dedicated to careers, more financially independent, and had most often been the ones to decide to walk when a marriage had become unbearable. Mothers of more than one kid were rarely the ones to leave, she found. Plus, mothers of onlies were more likely to move on to a new, healthy relationship. "In short," she wrote, "these women had adjusted well to their new roles as single mothers, and therefore they provided their children with an effective model for coping with the loss of an important family member."

The women Polit surveyed were comparable to divorced mothers in another survey ("By no means were we interviewing only successful adapters," she says). And while I've certainly heard about mothers like Amanda's, there have been many more stories about women described in terms that speak to Polit's study, if always in hindsight, years after the most intense post-divorce years. "My mother was awesome, she taught me how to cope with everything," one son tells me. "Hey, she's a survivor—a strong black woman, which is why I'm one too," says one daughter. "We were a team, but she was always my mother, and she never made me feel like she wasn't in control of her life or her choices—not for a second," I hear from another, who went on to become a powerful advocate for women's rights. "She made everything possible for herself, against all odds, and she also made everything possible for me." They describe intense relationships, like anyone else, but ones that modeled self-reliance.

Whether parents are single or coupled, many of us enjoy a quieter side to this intensity too; an unspoken intimacy. I remember as a child gingerly opening the door to my parents' bedroom, slashes of early morning light from the shutters setting the room softly aglow. I would tiptoe to the far side of the bed where my mother slept, and crawl under the paisley flannel duvet. Silently, I'd lay my head beside hers, and try to sync our breathing. Now I lie awake many mornings, awaiting Dahlia's cry of "Mama" before I creep into her room and lay my head on her pillow. She wriggles in close and takes hold of my elbow. And in the dark cocoon of her tiny room, I feel her try to sync her breathing with my own.

SIX

SAVE YOURSELF

I was trolling through Craigslist, looking for a secondhand Flexible Flyer wagon, when I idly clicked over to the vacation swaps. There it was: a loft in a garret by the Canal Saint-Martin, just a few blocks from where we had honeymooned for a week in a borrowed apartment. We knew the exquisite boulangerie on that very block. The couple—two men, one a trumpet player and one a medic who worked in a prison—were looking for a place in Brooklyn for a week. We had miles. We had wanderlust. We said yes. Some friends clucked that it would be too hard with Dahlia. ("A six-floor walk-up? Are you crazy?") Other rolled their eyes in camped-up jealousy. It was indeed a challenge, all those flights of stairs, her lunchtime fussiness gathering storms of scorn, the relentless effort to keep every one of their dust-caked tchotchkes out of her mouth (not to mention the lube collection by the bed we had to squirrel away). But we considered this a tiny price for those days of watching her play with French kids at playgrounds, marvel at the museums, and savor the caramel ice cream at Berthillon.

The second time Dahlia went to Paris, my parents had rented an apartment, making good on a lifelong promise to each other to spend a month there after retiring. (Rather, they made good on the Paris part of the promise—neither has found it worth kicking the work habit when it affords them, well, a rental in the Marais.) Dahlia came down with a stomach flu as we were boarding the plane and threw up, sitting on my lap, for the entirety of that dark transatlantic night. Her vomiting continued as we circled the city in a van—filled with a dozen tight-lipped other passengers—en route to the apartment. The next day, rosy cheeked and demanding pâte for lunch, she pointed to a fountain with a statue spouting water from its mouth and said, "That was me on the plane." That's when I taught my daughter the phrase, "Funny because it's true."

On that trip I met a woman named Michelle at a café in the shadow of the Pompidou. She was a former computer programmer in a sleeveless batik dress and African jewelry. Michelle's son, Pierre, now in college, went to school around the corner, where most of his classmates were only children like himself. "When Pierre was two, I spent a year thinking about it, whether to have another," Michelle says, stirring her café crème. "Now we can choose—so it becomes a problem since you have to decide, yes? I decided it wasn't possible for me. It was important for me to travel and take pictures. I worked, I was a mother, I had no time. I felt like I was a prisoner. A happy prisoner, but still a prisoner."

Despite that feeling, Michelle wondered if she should have a second, in case something tragic happened to Pierre—an impulse I've heard many parents admit. She even discussed this with a friend, a mother of four, whose oldest had nearly died in an accident. Her friend thought she was crazy. Michelle's husband wanted another, but he was passive about it. Eventually, she let the anxiety go. "I managed to do what I wanted to do," she says. "I've lived the life I wanted in my thirties, my forties, my fifties—they're all different lives, with different desires, which you never realize when you're young. I worked, I had a husband, I had a child. We traveled together. I took pictures. And Francis and I are still together—a very rare thing among people I know. You learn more and more that women don't do exactly what they want. You have to stay selfish. And it's hard to."

A 2007 Pew survey found that at a rate of nearly three to one, people believe the main purpose of marriage is the "mutual happiness and fulfillment" of adults rather than the "bearing and raising of children." Pew also found that only forty-one percent of today's adults see parenthood as very important to a success-ful marriage, down from sixty-two percent in 1990. If anything, it can be a detriment. The University of Chicago's Linda Waite, whose research focuses on how to make marriages last, tells me, "You're better off to ignore your kids and focus on your relation-ship than to focus on your kids and ignore your relationship," which she says few people have the courage to do. Instead, she says, we do the opposite. "*Kids, kids, kids.* That's how we forget about our own needs—it's all about *them.* And no one is happy like that."

What my mother needed to be a happy person is not what all mothers need. She needed to feel she was making a significant contribution through her work, and not just her family, work-ing for more than the necessary paycheck. She needed to live somewhere where she could walk a few blocks to buy a really good cookie when she got the craving after dinner. She needed to travel, to make her marriage as significant as her motherhood, to be able to go supermarketing and pick up the dry cleaning without being outnumbered by her kids, plural, who were performing the theater of rivalry in the produce section. I remember errands without another kid to help me make my case that carob was not the same as chocolate. I had no yard to play in. Was I a happy kid? Sure. Was she a happy mother? I think so.

Dahlia is home sick from school. She's dancing in a tutu from my second grade recital, its orange, green, and pink ruffles now rediscovered and tugged over her monkey pajamas. At her insistence (and my pleasure), I too am wearing a tutu—a can-can skirt I saved from junior high, pulled up over my jeans. She twirls and jumps between the pocket doors to our bedroom. This is what I imagined when I first saw our house, that these doors would make a perfect proscenium for living room performances. We spin together and wave our hands like the mice in the video of the Baryshnikov *Nutcracker* that is her longtime obsession. I tell myself to remember this. Then I look at the clock, remember the workday is in full swing, and scramble up to check my email.

There I see a note from a demographer; if I can call him now, he's free for an interview. I bellow downstairs for Justin to abandon the paperwork he's doing in favor of the next installment of *Nutcracker* mice and scurry out to my office clutching my frilled skirt around me. I dial up Philip Morgan at the Carolina Population Center, eager to hear his analysis of the recent study he conducted on our cultural notions of ideal family size. He parses a bevy of numbers that all add up to his summary that nobody wants just one kid, not anywhere, not even in Europe, where fertility rates have plummeted. Morgan is clinical and abrupt, circling back to the numbers whenever I attempt to talk about our cultural biases, our politics, what we see on TV. I explain to him

that I am an only child by design and that the small child pranc-
ing in a tutu in my house may well be one too.

"Listen, no offense to your mother or to yourself," he says, "but
I had three sons and I'm glad they have brothers. One of the most
enjoyable things I did as a parent was to watch my kids interact
with one another, hanging out, seeing them as adults interacting."
I am silent. He continues, "I can't imagine having just one child.
What would that be like? Their relationships with each other have
been the greatest joy of my life." I get it. I do. All I have to do is see
our friends' kids—plural—playing together, caring for each other,
sharing a secret language. All I have to do is watch Dahlia's joy and
tenderness when she gets to hold their baby brothers and sisters.
Justin sees it too, and he knows what she's missing. But he reminds
me often how the sacrifices we'd need to make to raise another
child would impact Dahlia's happiness—not to mention our own.

Robin Simon of Wake Forest University surveyed well-being
data from 13,000 respondents and, in a 2005 issue of *The Journal
of Health and Social Behavior*, published her findings that adults
with children experience depression and unhappiness in greater
numbers than non-parents. That's regardless of class, race, or
gender. Simon understands this phenomenon as a ruthless combination of social isolation, lack of outside support, and the anticipation of the overflow of bliss that we believe is the certain
outcome of every birth. "Our expectations that children guarantee
a life filled with happiness, joy, excitement, contentment, satisfaction, and pride—are an additional, though hidden, source of stress
for all parents," she wrote in *Contexts* magazine, adding, "negative
emotions may also lead parents with children of all ages, especially
mothers, to perceive themselves as inadequate since their feelings
aren't consistent with our cultural ideal." Right on, sister.

I find that parenting offers an untold bounty of happiness,
joy, excitement, contentment, satisfaction, and pride—just not all
the time. Each child is an additional source of pride, sure, but also
an additional infringement on freedom, privacy, and patience. I
can understand why Jean Twenge, in a study on parenthood and
marital satisfaction, found that happiness in a marriage tumbles
with each additional child. This finding bears out worldwide and
not just in the United States. Demographer Mikko Myrskylä
discovered that in some regions, like southern Europe, happiness
was also significantly higher among parents with one child. At a
demographic conference, Myrskylä tells me about the immense
pleasure he takes in his two children—though he's known to put
in longer hours at work these days, he says, since it feels "like a
holiday" after being at home.

At that conference, a young researcher named Anna Ba-
ranowska presents a paper giving additional heft to the finding
that one child may maximize personal happiness. The first child
tends to spike happiness in a parent, she declared, while every
subsequent child lowers it. In fact, social scientists have surmised
since the 1970s that singletons offer the rich experience of parenting without the consuming efforts that multiple children add:
all the miracles and shampoo mohawks but with leftover energy
for sex and conversation. The research of Hans-Peter Kohler, a
professor of demography at the University of Pennsylvania, and
Jere Berman, a professor of economics, gives weight to that idea.
In their much-discussed analysis of a survey of 35,000 Danish
twins, women with one child said they were more satisfied with
their lives than women with none or more than one. As Kohler
tells me, "At face value, you should stop at one child to maximize
your subjective well-being."

Then again, Kohler's wife was pregnant with his third child when he conducted his study, and he says his family is very happy. Of course, it all depends on what constructs your subjective well-being. That's, well, as subjective as it comes. When University of Pennsylvania demography professor Samuel Preston was conducting research to help him predict the future of fertility, the discovery that surprised him most was that parents fell so madly in love with their first child that they wanted a second. I am not someone who spent my first three decades imagining a glowing pregnancy followed by maternal bliss. In fact, I used to suspect that mothers who talked about their children with such unbridled awe didn't have much else going on in their lives. Then I had my daughter. Now I pull out my iPhone to show off pictures like the rest of them.

I don't believe that Kohler's research will tell me how to be happy any more than it told him. And I don't think Philip Morgan should be anything but thrilled with his three boys any more than I think Hillary Clinton should have been baking cookies at the White House—or giving Chelsea a sibling—when her subjective well-being depended on so many extra-domestic factors. We can't do much more than know ourselves.

Even though Robin Simon found that people with kids report higher levels of depression than those without, they also "derive more purpose and meaning in life than adults who have never had children." Is happiness a result of finding purpose and meaning? Is it the absence of depression? I'd contend it has a lot to do with having the freedom to live the life you want to live, whether that means five kids, or one, or none at all. To broaden out even more, Mikko Myrskylä discovered that the lower the overall fertility of the society, the happier are those who have children compared to those without. In a working paper for the

Max Planck Institute for Demographic Research, he offered the following analysis: in lower fertility cultures, the people who most want to have a child do—and they have only as many as they want—whereas in higher fertility societies, "Social pressure forces a less select group of people to have children." In other words, when people can make choices based on their own desires rather than what the world is telling them to do, the entire well-being of a society floats a little higher.

"What's so great about work anyway? Work won't visit you when you're old. Work won't drive you to get a mammogram and take you out after for soup. It's too much pressure on my one kid to expect her to shoulder all those duties alone. Also, what if she turns on me? I am pretty hard to like. I need a backup." So wrote Tina Fey in the final chapter of her book *Bossypants*, titled "What Should I Do with My Last Five Minutes?" The chapter is about, as she puts it, how her "last five minutes of being famous are timing out to be simultaneous with my last five minutes of being able to have a [second] baby." After she submitted her final draft to her editor, Fey opted to breed again, but not until providing us with a rare glimpse into the inner monologue of fertility ambivalence. It goes something like this, she wrote: "Should I? No. I want to. I can't. I must. Of course not. I should try immediately."

It's those "Last Five Minutes" that are key. As people increasingly put off child rearing—searching for the right relationship, satisfying work, a sense of readiness, none of which is guaranteed to be found—the relative freedom of preparenting adulthood contrasts even more madly with what Justin and I call the "new normal" of life under lockdown with a kid. We used to joke about how great it would be if we could get one of those cat feeders on a timer and fill it with applesauce, or find a baby monitor with a range that would stretch to the nearest bar. He and I are lucky to share both a sense of humor about parenting and a desire not to stretch ourselves to a fragile membrane just to provide a sibling for Dahlia. Not every couple is so aligned in these choices, even if they're ambivalent ones.

The practice of making a mutual life of both adventure and cozy domesticity has soldered us together over all these years. We know how parenting unavoidably shifts the balance of that equation, and we feel it acutely—if often pleasurably—having spent years that were weighted in the other direction. Jean Twenge believes that the sudden and ongoing loss of control over one's life, after we've had so much of it for so many years, underscores the uptick in dissatisfaction with parenting. "It's all about delayed fertility," Twenge tells me. "You had this time to live your life; you know what you're missing. When you've traveled the world or been in the boardroom, or even just had a regular job and had the freedom to eat lunch when you want to—it's an acute shock, and many people never get over it."

Having waited until my midthirties to have a kid, I know this well. To be sure, motherhood hasn't magically cured me of my desire to go to parties and rock shows. But Twenge says the very same culture that is insisting we have more babies is also delivering some crazy doublespeak. "You're supposed to be able to have it all—all the kids, all the freedom, and no compromises," she says. "Like, when I talk to people about reality"—the reality that you can't devote your entire life to a career, as well as parenting, as well as leisure; something's gotta give—"they say, 'you're telling us to give up on our dreams; you want us to settle.' People say, 'I will never compromise'—that's the essence of the problem."

I can't tell you how many conversations I've had in which people tell me they didn't "choose" to have an only child, though they did choose to try to conceive for the first time after their fortieth birthday. Delaying one's fertility usually means making the choice to have fewer children. I'm all for self-actualization. I'm all for the achievement of women in the marketplace. I'm all for signing on for this madness with the right partner. I'm all for putting it off until you think it's the right time. But in most cases, if you haven't tried to have a second child before your body timed out, that's a choice you've made. A tough one, and one you might feel something akin to regret about. But life choices tend to be made sequentially, this one as much as any other.

As long as the parent of a singleton is branded as selfish, people will have reason to take the defensive tack that it wasn't a choice they made. If we could eradicate the social stigma that stubbornly clings to the parents of only children, this defensiveness would disappear as well. So might the anxiety-laden behaviors that it yields. Carol Graham, who researches happiness and the family at the Brookings Institution, tells me, "The later people postpone fertility, the more they dive in hook, line, and sinker. They've got to do everything for their kids." Guilt, she reminds me, is a powerful motor. And at the same time, the farther we advance in our careers, the tougher it is on us to devote our energies elsewhere. No wonder psychologist Mathew White at the University of Plymouth has found higher levels of depressive symptoms among women who feel they have sacrificed their work for their families.

All of this adds up to a new level of angst, especially within the demographic that delays fertility the longest, the people who are higher achieving than ever: white American women. They are far more miserable than their mothers were, according to Andrew Oswald, an economist who studies happiness at the University of Warwick. "Highly educated American women are supposed to do it all—they're supposed to have all the virtues and accomplishments of their grandmothers but be an editor at a fashion magazine or run their own successful advertising companies," he tells me. (My mind prompts the *Dead Poets Society* chant, "Gotta do more, gotta be more.") Our expectations for success and happiness have become so supersized, as Twenge says, "it's gotten to a level of delusion."

Workaday achievement is insufficient; we aim for Fortune 500 achievement. And in our "pursuit of happiness," perhaps the greatest marketing slogan ever penned, written right into our Declaration of Independence, even happiness isn't enough; we expect euphoria. Anything less is compromise, which is anathema to Americans in particular. "This unwillingness to compromise is built into our individualism," says Twenge. Oswald, who is English, says that just because other countries aren't quite as single-mindedly triumphalist as we are, it doesn't mean European women have found the secret to bliss. They're increasingly more miserable as well, he points out, just not in big American portions of unhappiness. "We're all in this together in Western society," he says.

When I ask Oswald about Kohler's study that suggests stopping at one kid might provide a cure to some of this angst, he says it makes sense to him, not that it's the choice he and his wife made. Clinically, statistically, he says there's nothing but support for singletons as the way to balance the profound pleasures of parenting with some semblance of a liberated adulthood. "No one's going to tell you otherwise," he tells me. But who is making fertility choices based on statistics? As Alaka Malwade Basu noted in *Population and Development Review*, demographers have "overstated rationality at the expense of emotions." Instead, we lie awake at night thinking, as Tina Fey did, "Do I want another baby? Or do I just want to turn back time and have my daughter be a baby again?" I think this often. Many people I've interviewed admit the same.

We yearn for more parenting, for less parenting, for more work, for less work, for more pleasure—well, never for less pleasure. As a mother named Diana says reflectively when we meet at a bar in Berlin, "When does the yearning for more stop? It never stops. It doesn't stop with a husband. It doesn't stop with a better job. It doesn't stop with more money. It doesn't stop with a second child. This is life." She pauses to take a sip of dark beer and shakes her head. "I have to reconsider my notions of fulfillment. We all do. So we can be more faithful to ourselves." I think of something that Joan Didion, who happened to be the mother of an only child, wrote in one of the great defenses of selfishness as emancipation from other people's standards: "To free us from the expectations of others, to give us back to ourselves—there lies the great, singular power of self-respect."

At a recent gathering of single-child families in New Jersey, the selfish question comes up. Every woman at the table—some of whom had gone to expensive, debilitating lengths to conceive again—recounts being accused of selfishness by family members and strangers alike for not having a second child. Not a single man can offer up an equivalent story. One, a salesman in a pink oxford shirt and tie, says with smirking self-awareness, "Why would anyone say anything to me? I'm the father." Mothers are the ones who face the accusation. Both fathers and mothers pay dearly for the miracle of parenthood, but in most cases, it's women who pony up for the bulk of those costs.

The morning following that dinner in New Jersey, the Census Bureau released a report on who provides care for our children. Suzanne Bianchi, who clocked in sixteen years as a Census demographer, discovered, stunningly, that mothers actually spend *more* time caring for a child today than they did in 1965, back when sixty percent of them stayed home full-time. In her book *Changing Rhythms of American Family Life*, Bianchi wrote that married mothers devote about thirteen hours a week to child care, up from about ten and a half hours nearly a half century ago. Additionally, she wrote, women still do twice as much housework as men.

The parental breakdown of cleaning, cooking, bathing, playing, disciplining, story reading, and so on is an exceptionally well-studied area. Surveys have circulated in just about every demographic, statistics gathered and analyzed, papers presented. And yet the results are remarkably even. One study found that fathers provide twenty-eight percent of active care. Another declared that mothers provide more than two-thirds of care for kids under twelve. A third asserted that when both parents work fifty-two hours a week, women commit an additional thirty-three hours a week to "nonmarket" work; men get it up for only twenty hours of dishwashing and homework supervising. That's just in the United States, which doesn't even break into the top thirty in a study that ranked 134 countries by gender parity. It's worse in France, where women do eighty-nine percent of housework and child care (who has time to get fat on a treadmill like that?). Not a single survey contradicts the finding that when women increase their work hours, they never decrease the time they spend caring for and cleaning up after their kids. "They seem to do *more* housework, as if to compensate for their departure from traditional gender norms," says economist Nancy Folbre. No wonder Mikko Myrskylä, in his 2011 Max Planck paper on global happiness and fertility, found that "women experience greater stress and stronger negative shocks in well-being" than men after becoming parents. And just as none of this is good for women, none of it is good for a workforce.

Over *doppelmokkas* at Vienna's Café Sperl, Swedish demographer and feminist scholar Gerda Neyer explains to me that in Scandinavia—and to a slightly lesser extent, throughout Europe—family policy emerged as a labor movement concept. It was about workers' protection, not women's protection. France, for example, found itself in perennial worker shortages, so the only choice was to employ wives. Today Europe's panic over low fertility may be motivating policies, but the labor movement provided the foundation. "If Europe ever did anything good, it was the concept of the welfare state," she quips.

The concept of the noble worker has long extended to both sexes in Europe. Anne Solasz, at the Institut National Etudes Démographique in Paris, has three children, and it wouldn't occur to her not to spend her days at the office. "Women don't want to be at home here. They want to be employed not just for money but for agency, for freedom. It's healthier for me to work," she tells me. And she says the French state does everything to support that choice. This, after all, is a state that has recently announced it wants to shift the focus on the nation's success from GNP to "well-being," and therefore the engagement of mothers in a productive life outside the home is a significant factor in what policy makers are calling "happiness sustainability." In France the public holds negative attitudes to full-time mothering, which demographer Laura Bernardi has demonstrated in her own research. Widespread scorn for women who overthrow career for motherhood is how Solasz describes the reigning cultural conversation about "*le conflit*."

"I have all the child care I'd want, great free schools—it's the adult's life that leads family choice here, not the child's," Solasz tells me, sitting under a bulletin board pinned with her children's drawings. "And while women still have to do everything at home, it's still totally doable," she says, because she can drop off her kids before work and pick them up after, and not sign over her entire salary for the privilege. It's less doable in Italy and Germany, she comments—both countries that have opted for subsidizing domestic duties with cash payments rather than establishing free child care centers and other systemic solutions. "Which is why only children have become more normative there than here. When it's so much harder to have more kids, why would anyone do it?" Solazs asks.

Recent US studies show that men are doing more, at least—a third more than they did in 1965—but that doesn't mean it's making life easier for women. Things are just harder for everyone now. When the Families and Work Institute asked about 1,300 men if they were having a hard time juggling it all, sixty percent of men said they were struggling with the demands of work and family. The ever-deepening work-life conflict is a major factor explaining why nearly every country in the Western world reports declining levels of happiness—among both men and women. "No one wants to acknowledge the tradeoff, but there's always an argument about who does what, and there's always the potential for more argument in this crazy division of parenting roles," Folbre says. No wonder when Daniel Kahneman asked nine hundred working women to assess their daily experiences, one of the only things they said they enjoyed less than minding their kids was cleaning up after them. *Science* magazine may have made headlines when it reported his findings in 2004, but the misery of such drudgery is as old as dirt itself. As Simone de Beauvoir bemoaned in *The Second Sex,* "Few tasks are more like the torture of Sisyphus than housework, with its endless repetition. The clean becomes soiled, the soiled is made clean, over and over, day after day."

In my own household, Justin happily shoulders equal, or more, of the burden. This amazes friends. They ask me how I managed to get him with the program, as though it was a question of whipping a rogue horse into shape. My answer is simple: "If you want equal parenting, have a kid with someone who wants it even more than you do." They laugh and treat my statement as a hyperbolic quip. The fact is, I couldn't be more serious.

I know how unmanageable it all is with just one child. And I know how, when I mention this, people with two (or more) shoot disdainful looks in my direction, as if I'm bitching about my permanent vacation. "It's like hearing a skinny person complain about looking fat, and I don't want to hear it," one mother of two once snapped at me. There's no doubt about it: they have it harder. Much harder. Yet I've heard plenty of people tell me they think it's easier with siblings. "They take care of each other," they say on good days. I yearn for that missing element in my own home, not just for the pleasure of seeing Dahlia play with a little brother or sister, but for the moments of freedom it would allow me. But just as often, on bad days I hear, like I did from a friend last week, "Forget what I said about how they take care of each other. They're at war, my house is a mess, and I'm losing my mind."

While it's tough to measure the exact hours of sibling conflict a parent must referee, there exists some data to measure how
much tougher each additional kid can be. At the University of
Michigan, Frank Stafford runs the Panel Study of Income Dynamics, which is essentially a time diary that measures quantifiable aspects of our multitudinous lives. One category he follows
is housework. He finds this category so clear and reliable that
he uses it as the example when teaching people how to read his
complex tables. What he has learned is that this "labor in its
most naked state" increases dramatically with each child introduced into a household. Each child adds no less than 120 hours
of housework a year. No wonder those mothers of siblings can't
stomach my complaints.

But the issue today isn't as simple as washing sippy cups and
dirty socks, or even the sheer number of hours we spend away
from our friends and our thoughts. As the demands of the workplace have expanded to swallow up our lives, clashing with our
consuming love affair with our children, parenting has simultaneously morphed into something grotesquely extended beyond
traditional ideas of care. It's hard to imagine how anyone can find
time to make a living. Or read a newspaper. Or have a conversation with one's partner about anything but what errands need to
be done, who is covering pickup or making dinner.

"The mismatch in work and family balance creates a sense of
guilt and personal failure in the States," Tamar Kremer-Sadlik
tells me from her office at the UCLA Center on Everyday Lives
of Families. She has done a comparative self-reported diary study
of hundreds of Italian families and American families that lays
bare some sources of this mismatch. "The equivalent in Italian

data is to say, *well, that's life*. Laugh it off. There is no measuring stick in Italy for whether you're a good parent, and a good person. American mothers think they're individual failures because they see every issue as their own individual problem, not a structural problem." Kremer-Sadlik believes with no social support to pitch in, American parents feel extraordinary pressure to do everything it takes to get a child into the ever-shrinking middle class.

"I hear the anxiety," she tells me. "It's not just about overseeing homework. You work longer hours Monday through Thursday so you can volunteer at school Friday, which is the only way to get an edge, to know the teachers, to put your kid at an advantage at school." Then there's after-school sports, dance, music, language classes—not to help your kid become an outsized success, but only to maintain average status, since it's what everyone else is doing. This is what American adulthood looks like after children: the autonomy and agency of parents is ceded to our children. Indeed, according to University of Maryland time diary studies, women combine child care with their limited leisure time twice as much as they did in 1975.

"Why am I in traffic on Rockville Pike going to a Chuck E. Cheese birthday party for my whole Saturday? Because if everyone else's kid is doing it, your kid has to do it too," says Carol Graham at Brookings, who was raised in Peru by a Swiss mother. Both her research and personal experience suggest that emphasis on children is one of the major differences between families in America and those in other countries. "It's become a complete rat race. A million activities, practices every night. In other societies, kids fit into the family; parents are in charge," Graham tells me. "You don't walk into homes elsewhere and find the kid standing on the coffee table."

If you search for the term "family time" in American Google, Kremer-Sadlik points out, you'll find hundreds of thousands of entries. If you do it in Italian Google, she says, you'll find none. In their diaries, Kremer-Sadlik found, American parents wrote about Sea World, PG-rated movies, and turning down plans to make space for "family time"—meaning parents and kids doing something "kid oriented." Entries from Italian parents described dinner at eight, in the company of children, yes, but also friends with children, and even friends without children. In America, Kremer-Sadlik tells me, "Adults don't have a social life of their own; they don't hang out as *people*. It's an ideology here: when you have children, your world narrows down to your family. You shelter yourself from the outside world."

It's called "cocooning" when a family knits a translucent barrier between themselves and the rest of the world. I know how hard it can be to escape that isolation, even with one kid, and I have some of my dearest friends upstairs happy to come down for dinner at the drop of a text. Andrew Oswald tells me that beyond family, it's friendship networks that are most important and that the consuming nature of American parenting—on top of the consuming nature of American work—is what puts those networks in jeopardy. "The need of a second career within the home means friendship networks have to be dismantled, and that's risky to human happiness and mental health," he says. Alice Rossi and other researchers have found that American parents raise their children in greater isolation than their counterparts anywhere else, receiving little assistance from friends, extended family, and the larger community. And what community exists becomes defined by *children*—note the plural.

"When you have two children and two careers, that leaves

almost no time for parents to have same-sex friends or couple friends," psychiatrist Jacqueline Olds tells me in our conversation about loneliness. "Dinner parties are impossible, so you have to have a pizza party with a whole other family just to manage it at all. When it comes down to it, two children really outnumber parents." Olds herself has two: "I know—two kids have the power to knock the stuffing out of life." What happens, Olds tells me, is that the more isolated parents are from everyone except their children, the more they inadvertently rely on them for companionship. Demarcation between adults and kids fades. Children's needs and desires dictate the tenor and priorities of a home.

It's not just ballet and birthday parties. In certain zip codes especially, there's something deeper afoot. When I watch early seasons of *Mad Men*, the anachronism that always startles me isn't the three-martini lunch or the sexist workplace, but the one line mother Betty Draper barks more than any other: "Sally, go watch TV!" Show me a mother in the current-day Draper class who is comfortable parking her kid in front of the tube instead of embarking upon a craft project using post-consumer waste materials or heading out to a sustainable farm-to-table class for her toddler.

As Erica Jong wrote in a *Wall Street Journal* essay that led many expensively educated mothers to pen furious letters to the editor: "Unless you've been living on another planet, you know that we have endured an orgy of motherphilia for at least the last two decades." This motherphilia, "our new ideal," is characterized by "homemade baby food, cloth diapers, a cocoon of clockless, unscheduled time," Jong wrote, amounting to a "prison for mothers," or at least for mothers who can afford heirloom spelt flour and baby-and-me yoga classes.

—

"It's all the composting and cupcakes!" Linda Hirshman tells me, when we meet for lunch to parse how parenting has devoured us alive. Hirshman wrote a slim book called *Get to Work* a few years ago that made Jong's *Wall Street Journal* essay look like the work of Phyllis Schlafly. She had noticed that *The New York Times* wedding announcements had become a parade of hypereducated brides who were jettisoning their promising and hard-won, if relatively nascent, careers in favor of the trappings of domestic life. These were the smiling faces—all that good orthodontic work— of the so-called opt-out revolution. *Get to Work* was a data-driven, philosophically grounded response to their ilk. Women who have relinquished their role in the marketplace for a life of wearing yoga pants to school pickup, she observed, "are dependent on the productivity and continuing goodwill of the men they married. They cannot support themselves or their children. They cannot decide where their family is going to live." (I'd add, God help them if they join the half of wives who get divorced.) The outcome, she wrote, "robs not just these women of their own power, but in the aggregate, becomes a sex-specific brain drain from the future rulers of our society."

Hirshman was not alone in witnessing this brain drain. About a decade ago, Harvard Business School professor Myra Hart found that only thirty-eight percent of mothers with Harvard MBAs were working full-time. Census figures for mothers with graduate degrees and small children show that only half work full-time. These are what a friend of mine calls "uptown problems." It's not like these women are being pushed out of the workplace. And these uptown girls are also the mothers least likely to carry the water for their entire families. It's the women without degrees, holding lower paying jobs, who are the ones doing everything at home. Demographer Livia Oláh has found that worldwide, highly educated parents are far more likely to equally share child-care responsibilities.

But for rich women and poor women alike, the more children a woman has, the less likely she is to maintain her employment—and, consequently, her independence. Even two is often too much. In *The Price of Motherhood*, Ann Crittenden wrote, "The most popular form of family planning in the United States and other wealthy countries—two children, spaced not too far apart—is incompatible with most women's careers. Even if a new mother and her employer can cope with one child, the second baby is often the final straw," she asserted. Countless mothers, Crittenden declared, found that the birth of a second baby, and the impossibility of arranging a short workweek to accommodate it, destroyed their careers." It's worth noting that Crittenden, whose own career has landed her at *The New York Times*, *Newsweek*, and *Fortune* as a reporter, CBS News as a commentator, MIT and Yale as a lecturer, and the Fund for Investigative Journalism as the executive director, is the mother of an only child.

We tend to consider female ambition a modern invention, circa shoulder pads and IUDs, pulling on our halos of hardwired maternal goodness until they snap in two. But as anthropologist and primatologist Sarah Blaffer Hrdy has pointed out, this halo was in fact a Victorian fabrication. Ambition, she says, is exactly what we're hardwired for. It's what a chimpanzee mother needs to keep other females from eating her offspring (and I thought the undermining parents at the playground were a tough crowd) or monopolizing resources she needs to feed her baby. Hard-won seniority, for mothers, means survival. Hrdy, in her fascinating book *Mother Nature*, wrote, "striving for local clout was genetically programmed into the psyches of female primates during a distant past when status and motherhood were totally convergent."

But, as Hrdy wrote, "most mothers reading this book worry far less about famine, tigers, and infanticidal conspecifics than they worry over job promotions, health benefits, and finding adequate daycare." Adequate day care is no less a threat to mothers today than tigers were to our primate ancestors. Hrdy volunteered that as her book went to press, her youngest child (of three) was twelve years old—and she still had live-in child care. Her rare ability to afford such help is what enables her to do her work, to be more than just a mother. Not that even with such an unusual level of support can she follow monkeys in India for weeks or months at a time, as she did before she had children. No wonder female scientists have fewer children than anyone else.

A survey tracking families from the late 1980s through the early 1990s showed that while a single child decreases a mother's employment by about eight hours a week, the second kid leads to a *further* reduction of about twelve hours. A father's work hours don't change at all when a first child is born, but an additional child actually *increases* his time on the job by about three hours per week. With all this in mind, Hirshman instructed readers (with her italics), "Have a baby. *Just don't have two*," citing Judith Stadtman Tucker of Mothers Movement Online, who asserts that women who opt out of work to care for kids usually do it only after the birth of a second child. As she wrote, "a second kid pressures the mother's organizational skills; doubles the demands for appointments; wildly raises the costs of child care, education and housing; and drives families to the suburbs," where, as she puts it, Chinese takeout is less of an option at the end of a crazed workday.

It's easy to see how additional kids add additional madness to our already mad world. During the past fifty-odd years, not only have the number of hours of child care increased, so has the average American workweek—by thirteen hours. In fact, though we have less state support for families, we have the longest workweek in the developed world. In Norway, land of universally subsidized child care, workers clock in 1,400 hours per year to our 1,900 hours. In fact, we spend more time at work than the citizens of any other industrialized country and all but two developing nations. While work hours have increased significantly here, they've consistently decreased in most other industrialized nations, according to the International Labor Organization. And as per a Berkeley study on "The Overworked American Family," each parent in a dual earner family works an average of fifteen hours a day on a combination of work and family chores.

It's not like the conflict between parenting and professionalism is anything new. Sarah Blaffer Hrdy considered how the tension between subsistence and reproduction is easily discerned among our evolutionary ancestors. Though they, as she says, "just lugged their babies through the forest while foraging—but we can't lug them through the factory." And though we become more educated, more technologically advanced, more psychologically astute, more vocal about our painful tradeoffs, things simply get worse. You can see why some mothers who can afford to would say *screw it* to a career.

But in recent surveys parents often describe the workplace as less stressful and more personally rewarding than the home. It's social, it's adult, it's results oriented—and often it seems to be the only place parents can escape the cacophony of their kids. When mothers don't work, they aren't just losing financial freedom and power but also equal daily participation in the adult world. That's a large part of why, in a recent Pew survey, ninety-one percent of people say the most satisfying kind of marriage is one in which both parents work. Or, rather, ninety-one percent of people in France say this—only seventy-one percent of Americans agree.

Traditional roles in the United States refuse to loosen their stubborn grip, regardless of the cost. Philip Morgan, the population researcher who can't imagine denying himself or his sons a family with three siblings, has written extensively on women "missing the target" of their intended family size, "which is almost never one child," though he admits this "doesn't have the negative effects we might imagine on happiness or other measures of well-being." I respond that when one asks an eighteen-year-old—as he does—what she imagines her future to hold, few probably conjure the compromises of adulthood. Or a thirty-year-old before she's had her first child. Or her first mortgage. Or a major deadline when her child has the flu.

One of the central myths of America is that we can engineer a life without tradeoffs. Ruled by such mythology, we're devastated by overcommitment and the isolation it yields, gasping for breath on a hamster wheel we stay on until we collapse. It takes a financial crisis to even consider reexamining our priorities, and at that point we're stretched too thin to do much about it. In our perceived powerlessness some of us withdraw into the home to attempt to seize control over some sphere of our lives—the tiny universe we've attempted to build on our own terms.

This is especially true once you abandon the city for the suburbs, where one's private realm replaces a public sphere that no longer exists, Andres Duany, coauthor of *Suburban Nation*, tells me. Today's houses are "fully equipped to compensate and mitigate the loss of the public realm," he says. Fifty years ago homes averaged 1,700 square feet. Now that figure is up to 2,700, and interior architecture, in Duany's mind, exists to mimic an urban world where few Americans dwell today. The double-height entry hall is the surrogate of the town square; the media room supplants the theater; the master suite practically exists as its own town house. Multiple dining areas further service our separation from the outside world: the breakfast nook is the diner; the formal dining room is the special-occasion white-tablecloth restaurant; even the kitchen island functions like a European tabac. "If you had a public realm," Duany says, "you wouldn't have to buy more house" for more children.

There's a reason, he tells me, that suburban adulthood is such a fiercely isolating experience. Forget the loneliness of the only child; not only are we sequestered in our homes—when we're not at a child's event—we spend so much of our lives in cars, suspended in our steel and glass bubbles, rushing to and from school, to and from soccer, and to and from work. Sure, French mothers might do eighty-nine percent of housework. But when they are asked to rate how much they're always putting kids' needs before their own, it turns out they're half as likely as American mothers to suggest they deny their own needs. I suppose it follows that in a survey comparing the happiness of mothers in France and Texas, *les meres* say they're quite content during the time they spend with their children. The Texans rank those moments of their days below the misery of commuting.

Larger families demand more living space, which becomes more affordable the farther you get from urban centers. In 2008 Swiss economists Alois Stutzer and Bruno Frey found that while people gladly trade a longer daily commute for a sizable house in the suburbs, there exists a direct link between long drives to work and low well-being. In fact, they reported that people who commute roughly forty-five minutes each day have to earn nineteen percent more a month than they already do to make the trip worthwhile. We work more to support bigger families in bigger houses and bigger cars—and then we regard our families as a source of duty rather than pleasure. All of this surely slams up against a culture that promotes more breeding. Furthermore, if we're just following the social road map, why are we blaming ourselves for our unhappiness?

We may not have the time or energy to organize and participate in movements for social change, or even read the newspaper, but we can bake organic cupcakes and supervise algebra homework and spend our lives driving from soccer to ballet and watch Nick Jr. in our media rooms. All that overparenting seems selfless for a reason: parents are literally *losing themselves*. Our communities and democracy are losing them too. Imagine if all that devotion wasn't just directed inward to the family, but outward into the world? It's hard to, isn't it? The world can sound and look remarkably hazy from inside a domestic cocoon.

SEVEN

HOME ECONOMICS

In a leafy outdoor café in Berlin, Catherine, an American-born singleton, agonizes to me about her IUD. It's been ten years since her son, an only child as well, was born. She has to get it taken out. Does she get another one? She's only thirty-seven. Germany gives her 189 euros a month for her son, who goes to school at a wonderful public gymnasium (she spent her childhood in New York and Boston's best private schools and says his is easily as good) and has fantastic after-school programs also provided by the state. "Oh my god, it is *so* much easier for us," Catherine says. "They're just handing us money to make more Germans." And yet, Germany's total fertility rate is currently 1.4 births per woman. Austria's is the same. In both countries single-child families have become an accepted norm, says Joshua Goldstein, who heads up the Max Planck Institute for Demographic Research in Rostock. "This 'only child problem' you Americans perceive, this stereotype—we just don't have it here," a Belgian demographer tells me over coffee in Vienna one snowy afternoon. "And if we ever did, we surely don't have it anymore. The issue here isn't only children, it's no children at all."

In Europe, parenthood has become a massive political issue. Panic over low fertility has swelled into a wave of family policies that range from mandated paternity leave to guaranteed child care from infancy to cash payments for every birth. Or, I should say, native European fertility: Muslim immigrants have defused what Nicholas Eberstadt at the American Enterprise Institute calls Europe's "depopulation bomb" with their high birth rates. White, educated citizens have simply gone on birth strike, recoiling from the sacrifices that children require, and without a strong church to dictate otherwise. Even with higher immigrant fertility in the mix, southern European women are breeding at fraulein rates of 1.4 children. In Eastern Europe the numbers are even lower.

To put it simply, governments from the Mediterranean to the Baltic Sea have freaked out—and in most of the world, that is what it takes to develop extensive family policy that reconciles the realities of motherhood with the requirements of modernity. The 2010 European Union summit in Barcelona decreed that member nations must provide child care for a minimum of thirty-three percent of children under age three and ninety percent between three and the local legally required school age. This is on top of the preexisting parental leave directive of three months at full pay for both mothers and fathers. Unsurprisingly, a spate of research has shown that these policies have a positive effect on gender relations.

You could see all this as feminism, but really, it's economics—and racial anxiety. Demographers and sociologists have been deployed en masse to figure out how to get native Europeans to have more babies. Thus an academic area that initially had drawn a generation of researchers into developing countries to figure out how to get poorer dark-skinned women to have *fewer* kids has shifted its focus to helping richer, light-skinned women have *more* kids. Of course, demographers insist that it's all led by the same goal: to help women live the lives that they want. Most of us women could have told researchers what we need in order to pursue more fulfilled and manageable adulthoods, without commissioning copious quantitative studies. We need more time, and we need more money.

A roster of star demographers convenes annually at the Vienna Institute of Demography's conference at the Austrian Academy of Sciences. Down a tiny, snow-packed pedestrian lane, through an antique wooden double door, and up worn marble stairs, the setting for this conference is as gloriously Old World as it gets. Under a chandelier and trompe l'oeil painted ceilings, a Bulgarian demographer declares the goal of the gathering: "To drive policy that will change birth rates." I'm amazed that during the days that we're gathered here, no one seems to question whether we actually *want* more children.

On my way to the academy each morning, I pass families pulling their small singletons to school in toboggans through this snow-kissed fairyland, aware that even though superior public support exists here, thirty percent of Austrian families still stop at one kid. I'm jealous as hell of parents who receive *kindergeld,* or have terrific child-care centers they can drop their kids off at while they go participate in the adult world—without having to compare the cost of each hour of child care with the money earned during that hour. If I lived in a country where policy was more conducive to having another child, so I would not have to so radically reshape the life I've worked hard to build for myself, perhaps Dahlia would have a little sister or brother right now. I think of a physician's assistant I met shortly before my flight to Vienna—a woman from France raising an only child in Brooklyn. "If I was still in France I'd have at least another, but here? *Pffhh.* It's impossible."

Beyond minimum requirements the EU sets to help families, policy is different all over Europe, and the group gathered here has found that each country's attempt to solve *le conflit* is directly related to how many kids a family feels it can handle. For example, in southern Europe, where governments write checks for new babies without establishing systemic solutions for their care, the total fertility rate is still the lowest on the continent. In Scandinavian countries where services are universal, assuring children the right to such care, fertility is the highest. Nordic countries may have been hit hard by the global recession, but their child care and health care, defined as a right, go untouched despite budget slashing in other government offices. Even recent extensive leave policies have not infringed on the requirement that every child have access to full-time day care. When I comment to Europeans here that there is almost no discussion of the need for such policies in the United States, they're stunned.

Everywhere in Europe are the ghosts of the twentieth century. Grueling hardship is hardly a generation removed. In Germany I met an only child named Antje who grew up on the east side of the Wall, where as a kid she had owned one puppet and two books. Her mother would tell her the stories she remembered from her own childhood; "Her stories were my books," she says. She remembers her mother waiting in a line for three days for trousers for her daughter. "We were all only children," Antje tells me. "How could it be any other way? There was no time.

Everyone worked all the time. Everything was too impossible." Antje's mother loved to travel before Germany was divided, so she gave her daughter a name from Holland, her favorite place, which she assumed Antje would never be permitted to see.

Now Antje has a job she loves, running communications for a luxury hotel, and travels at every opportunity, seizing freedom with a vengeance. She doesn't want to sacrifice the experience of motherhood, but she doesn't want to yield entirely to it either. So she says she'll probably stop at one. Indeed, former Communist countries still have some of the lowest fertility anywhere, just behind East Asia. "Only children are what's normal to me," Antje says, fiddling with a diamond pendant her mother could have never imagined around her neck. "Sure, things are much better than they were, but that doesn't mean it's not still hard, and it doesn't mean we don't know better."

It would have been hard to imagine in the postwar years that one day raising a child in the United States could require more sacrifice than raising one in the kindergartens of Europe. According to the USDA, a child born in 2010 will cost an average of $226,920 to raise to age eighteen. Forget college, that doesn't even enter into it. The high price of children is rising at a considerably higher rate than inflation; during the relative boom of the year 2000, the USDA figure was $165,630. And if you factor in the opportunity costs of a mother's loss of income—accounting for parental leave, scaling back work hours, and other aspects of so called "mother penalties" in our winner-take-all workforce— you're looking at more than a million dollars. That figure doesn't come from a feminist think tank study (though plenty can back it up with hard figures), but from a conversation I had with Bryan

Caplan, an economist and the pronatalist author of *Selfish Reasons to Have More Kids.*

Yet Caplan believes that despite all we know, "big families are more affordable than ever, because we're more than three times richer than we were in 1950." Sure, he says, "women lose more income when they take time off, but they also have a lot more income to lose." I don't see how such a rationale forgives what the Institute for Women's Policy Research recently learned: over fifteen years of "prime-age" working, women earned only thirty-eight percent of men's wages, principally due to cutting back hours for caregiving. Caplan argues nonetheless that "today's parents have money to throw around at problems great and small," and that "thanks to the growth of technology and wealth, parenting has never been less laborious or more affordable." Lambasting our motherphilia, Caplan urges that we use our televisions as babysitters.

In some ways I'm with him—and after speaking to him, I felt much better about sending Dahlia off to school that morning in a dress over her pajamas. His thinking, which echoes a rationale I've heard from many parents of siblings, is that once you make the upfront investment of time and money in one child, the rest is nothing. In truth, your first child is your most expensive. But it's hardly like you're picking up the rest at Sam's Club. Consider these budgets from Nancy Folbre's book *Valuing Children*: A family that spends $11,000 on one child (and that's way, way below the national average) spends $18,000 on two. And yes, the third one is cheaper if you want to look at it that way, at $7,000 each, but it still adds up to $21,000. The differences between those totals are extreme, at least to my bank account. Resource dilution is also in play: a singleton in this equation receives the advantage of that full $11,000, whereas the siblings make do with a much smaller share; meanwhile parents must spend significantly more.

Two-parent households with two children devote over a third of their income to their kids. The percentage increases with each additional child, and, most troubling, the less parents earn. For example, the average family living in poverty pays forty percent of their income just to cover child care, compared to parents over the poverty line who shell out only seven percent of their wages. It's hard to imagine who Bryan Caplan is talking to when he writes about birthing babies. "As a consumer, how do you change your behavior when a product gets cheaper or better or easier to purchase?" he asks. "You buy more. You go back. You tell your friends. You post a five-star review on Amazon. If kids are the product, consumer logic still applies. Buy more as the deal gets sweeter." The notion of children as durable goods springs from the mind of Nobel Prize–winning economist Gary Becker. Becker's theory of economics contends that there's really no difference between deciding to raise a child and making any other investment. Kids, like anything else, he says, are a form of capital that yield a future flow of valuable services. Which, if you have land to work, makes perfect sense; less so, I'd say, in the modern world.

If that's how people make the choice to become parents, and to have additional children, I've yet to meet any. It strikes me as theoretical at best to compare the acquisition of, say, a front-loading washing machine with small and dependent people with charms, habits, frustrations, faces, voices, and so on. However you might identify the impulse to bring a child into your family, to love and tend a new and growing life, it's probably not a cost-benefit analysis. Children are a desire, not a calculation. Which is why I believe that if you truly desire more than one child, you'll make it work. People always have. And if you don't, well, there's a big stack of numbers on your side. If we're going to be rational about it, surely the economic verdict suggests we should stop at one.

It's absurd that in these dark economic days single-child families still have the reputation of being wealthy ones. Certainly, there has been a history of urbane parents whose only children have private-school pedigrees and stamp-filled passports. (I'm a relatively low-rent version of that sort of uptown girl, myself.) But the cliché falls apart, especially in a lousy economy. "Because kids are expensive, you buy less of them," as Elizabeth Ananat, assistant professor of public policy and economics at Duke University, sums up a body of research at the 2011 Population Association of America conference. At that conference, Kevin Mumford, professor of economics at Purdue University, presents data that directly contradicted the notion that only children come from wealthy families. Each $100,000 in household income, he says, raises fertility by ten to fourteen percent.

As a student loan crisis grows in the United States, this gyre will surely widen. For the first time, what students owe on their tuitions is greater than what the entire country owes on its credit cards. College diplomas awarded in 2010 came with an average of $24,000 in debt. Couple that figure with low employment and it's easy to see why an entire generation is facing delaying fertility, and curbing it, so finances can align with family plans.

And yet, the myth holds that only children are spoiled rich kids. When I interview British economist Andrew Oswald, he assumes that Justin and I would stop at one for "ski vacations and sports cars without baby seats." Tell that to Kathy and Shay, two product managers with one child, whose four-year-old daughter goes to Montessori school while they work. Over burgers at a New Jersey Fuddruckers, they tell me they've been thinking about another but can never figure out how to reconcile the child-care costs and, beyond that, the toll of parental responsibility. The expectations at her office are unrelenting, she says. "I work in the corporate world. It's a lot of men. They don't care about what I have to do at home." She stops midthought, watching a mother in yoga pants who is carrying one child on her hip and literally pulling two others past us. The mother closes her eyes against the whining behind her. Kathy shoots her a tight smile, and once the mother has passed our table, sighs and shakes her head.

A year into our current economic crisis, physicians reported a boom in permanent procedures like tubal ligations and vasectomies (though the latter can usually be reversed). Clinics could hardly keep up with the demand for Essure and IUDs. It's easy to understand why fertility plummets not just during unemployment, but in a housing bust, as Mumford presented at the conference. When you're forced to move back in with your parents, partner and dependent in tow, you're not thinking about making babies, as social psychologist Susan Newman explained in her book *Under One Roof Again*. Honestly, if we hadn't moved out of our small apartment during the boom, it's hard to imagine we'd have Dahlia today. I hate to think of her existence as mandated by timing in the real estate market, but what might have functioned as a nursery was my office and Justin's equipment closet. As it is, her current bedroom was initially a windowed dressing room.

One night Dahlia and I walked down the block for pizza (bless the gods of urban living), and while chatting over our slices, *CBS Evening News* comes on the television suspended over the counter. We sit transfixed by a segment on Slab City, where a massive community of homeless families have settled atop the acres of concrete that remain from abandoned World War II barracks. Dahlia chews thoughtfully as she watches a father tell the reporter about how he had worn a tie to work until six months ago, when he lost everything and had no choice but to move his three kids to this makeshift town in the California desert. Then she shifts her eyes to me, and asks, "Mama, that won't be us because there's only one of me instead of three?"

She's on to something. The basic math of what one child costs—in money, time, and energy—is something simple enough to intuit. What she doesn't know is that increasingly, the less money a mother has, the less likely she is to have a partner, even an unemployed one. Marriage, or even permanent copartnering outside of the legal definition, is becoming a line drawn between classes. It's one thing (though an eminently reasonable thing) to bitch about what husbands don't do and to voice concern about mothers fleeing the workplace when two partners share a household. But increasingly those two parents have become a luxury good. A majority of mothers under thirty without college degrees have children and no partner. Plenty of them started college but weren't able to afford what it takes—again in money, time, and energy—to graduate. Now they're parenting on their own. Think about what each additional kid costs and then imagine how that weight mounts on the shoulders of one person trying to do it all, alone. It will hardly stun you to learn that, invariably, in single-parent households the top expense is child care.

When the economy drops out, so does fertility. But the shrinking of families was probably never as drastically felt as it was in the thirties. Not only were we slammed under the boot heel of the Great Depression, but advents in industry, education, and philosophy had begun to radically redraw the scope, and purpose, of women's lives. Women's work became a necessity in the United States, and a requirement in the Soviet states. For good and for far worse, definitions of human purpose and potential were shifting as the financial viability of realizing any potential at all taunted most people. Yet ideas held strong of what a woman was, and what a family was.

In 1933 an illustration of a family of four, gathered around the hearth, accompanied William F. Ogburn's *New York Times* story on trends in "the American Family today." Ogburn wrote, "The time once was when a child was self-supporting on a farm by the time he was 10 years old." But in the industrialized age, children had become expenses rather than assets, he wrote, changing the shape of our families. And change it had: so common had single-child families become that I have in my kitchen a slim cookbook with a gorgeous orange art deco cover called *Cooking for Three*, published this same year. A new kind of family—and a new kind of mother—had arrived. In the 1930s, the single child rate rose to more than thirty percent of families.

During the Depression, the government established emergency nursery schools so women could go to work. But these were immediately shuttered as soon as the economy recovered (thanks, in large part, to the very women who were shuttled back to the kitchen). Then once the United States entered the Second World War, the state established day-care centers near defense factories where all those Rosies were required to rivet, costing each mother about fifty cents a day. But come V-Day, once more the notion of subsidized child care was instantly abandoned. Until 1971, that is, when Congress passed the Comprehensive Child Development

Act, a national day-care system designed to help single working mothers care for their children. Alleging that the policy smacked of woeful Communism and declaring it had a "family weakening implication," Nixon vetoed the bill as soon as it hit his desk. And so it goes. Or how it goes here, in the only country in the industrialized world that refuses to guarantee paid parental leave.

The United States has long claimed a national faith in the strength of our economy. And when you read books by people— usually men—on the relationship between our breeding and our banks, you'd think women who aren't pushing out two or more babies are burning flags (and bras) in our public squares. This is where the selfishness of the single-child parent is treated like treason, like we're shutting down the factories and sinking the stock market by the stagnant power of our underutilized wombs. Phillip Longman at the New America Foundation has named our low-breeding economic dystopia the "gray tsunami," the tidal wave that will wipe out America when the declining numbers of people under thirty have to support a disproportionately gray-haired population.

Europe's response to this anxiety, as we know, is to develop policies that lessen the burden of parenting, encouraging fathers to take advantage of paternity leave with financial support, urging mothers to align a role in the workplace with responsibilities at home. Meanwhile, the United States merely turns a blind eye to the circumstances of the modern family. Longman, whose voice rings the loudest in the alarmist debate about the relationship between birthrates and markets, has opined extensively about what he thinks is the best solution for the American future: a return to radical patriarchy. As he wrote in a 2006 essay in *Foreign Policy*,

"One must observe that a society that presents women with essentially three options—be a nun, be a prostitute, or marry a man and bear children—has stumbled upon a highly effective way to reduce the risk of demographic decline." This type of society, he believes, will save us from extinction. "Patriarchy made the incentive of taking a husband and becoming a full-time mother very high because it offered women few desirable alternatives," (see *nun, prostitute*) which leads to better parenting, he contends.

Longman does not just envision this system for Islamic populations, or the American Judeo-Christian orthodoxy. It's Europe and Japan, with their dramatically lowered birthrates, that will first "by a process similar to survival of the fittest, be adapted to a new environment in which no one can rely on government to replace the family, and in which a patriarchal God commands family members to suppress their individualism and submit to father." Rather than a tableau of certain hell, Longman asserts he's conjuring an image of our inevitable *salvation*. This, he says, is how we will begin to regenerate ourselves, and our economic future.

Discourse about the balance between fertility and prosperity has been exclusively pronatalist, usually quite backward looking, and, in my experience, almost never remotely interested in egalitarianism or policy initiatives. Still, the relationship between falling birthrates and falling economies is not a specious one. Let's take Japan as an example, as Longman does. The population there is expected to fall by one third by midcentury. Already, because of the large number of elderly citizens and the birth dearth of the young, the country—the ultimate example of late-twentieth-century wealth—has entered what Japanese academics have called the first low birthrate recession. It's become the cautionary tale of economy-minded natalists. The country is like a hyperkinetic version of the rest of us industrialized cultures, with a growing population of single adults, consumed with work and the pursuit of pleasure, delaying marriage and fertility, ambivalent about the personal costs of parenthood. In Asia, Japan has been at the vanguard of female autonomy. It also has more only children than almost anywhere else in the world (South Korea and Taiwan vie for that distinction).

But it's worth remembering how these fertility choices are made. People commit to each other at much later ages than they used to, dedicating their twenties, and often much of their thirties, to education, careers, and the pursuit of lasting love. Perhaps these committed partners will decide to have a child, after which they face the same dilemma the rest of us do when thinking about having another. Albeit with universal health care, financial support for families with a child under three, and an extensive national network of state-funded child-care centers.

At a tiny teahouse in Tokyo, a music magazine editor named Kotaro, an only child with an only child, tells me that we can talk about economics and policy all day, but in the end, that's not the point. He and his wife are discussing another kid, but he's deeply ambivalent. Not because she would have to work more to secure a place in public day care, or because it means he might need to find a better paying job, maybe one that wouldn't neatly hew to his oversized hooded sweatshirt and long hair. "The money doesn't matter so much. I think people do what they want anyway," he says.

What Kotaro wants is to read comic books with his first grader, Hana. She's currently obsessed with one called *Blackjack* about an unlicensed surgeon. After a long day at work and before a short night of sleep, he and Hana curl up on the couch with dark tales of bizarre symptoms, looking at grisly art of human organs. Kotaro says he and his wife would never consider having another child to boost the economy. I can't imagine anyone who would.

In the United States, Longman and other population-minded economists articulate the fear that our prosperity will implode when what he calls "America's vanishing labor supply" hits a crisis point, one we are nearing because women like me are producing fewer future members of the workforce. I find that this argument is gravely challenged by unemployment, but I've been told I'm too short minded. Yet so is a solution that demands more children and more women dropping out of the marketplace to raise them. All of us ladies working instead of looking after our kids contributes to economic growth. We earn a wage. We buy things. We increase the gross domestic product.

No doubt, the fewer kids we have, the older our population becomes. Compared to the average adult, children cost over a quarter less and the elderly cost over a quarter more, mainly because of health-care costs. Which means that declining fertility can give an economy a shot in the arm, as it did here in the seventies and eighties, but after a lag it contributes to economic stress, when there are fewer of us to support our grandparents. That's inarguable. Chinese singletons have already learned this the hard way in a country where the state offers little family support. As the social security coffers run dry, we're facing a similar story here.

Nicholas Eberstadt of the American Enterprise Institute has furrowed his brow a great deal over that "depopulation bomb" in Russia—which loses three-quarters of a million citizens a year—but he says even if it were to go off in the United States, we wouldn't face the same kinds of collective problems. "It's not like we don't have the social capital, the rule of law, the sorts of institutional infrastructure that we in the West take for granted," he tells me. He says he's not even that worried about Europe. Of course, at least when it comes to supporting families, Europe's institutional infrastructure makes our family values–governed one look like it was developed in the legislative quarters of a developing country.

In Germany the government is simultaneously debating austerity measures alongside a bill to offer an additional 190 euros a month to parents who want to hire in-home child care, or, if they want to save the money, provide it themselves. Activists have taken to dressing in vintage dirndls and hausfrau robes to protest the measure, since they believe it threatens to tether women to maternity rather than encourage them to live extra-domestic lives in the workplace. Countries with more conservative welfare regimes, such as Germany or Italy, see fewer women do wage-earning work after becoming mothers—especially the second time—than more liberal ones. The happiness rates track accordingly, with social democratic countries supporting the happiest parents on earth.

"Social democratic" does not mean "socialist," it means a capitalist structure committed to supporting its citizenry as well as its economy. Philip Longman and other thinkers of his ilk contend that low fertility stifles capitalism. He points out to me that historically, "capitalism has never flourished except when accompanied by population growth." Capitalism in its purest, most ideological form is the market religion of self-interest. Yet many women around the world have come to understand that bigger families are not necessarily in their own self-interest.

Most of us have rejected the binaries of mother versus wage earner (just as we've long shelved nun versus prostitute). Perhaps these doomsaying economists can one day reject the binary of capitalism versus socialism as well, so our systems can support everyone, not just paterfamilias.

EIGHT

THE FRUITFUL MANDATE

Americans make enough babies to maintain replacement fertility, an average of more than 2.1 children per woman. However, this national figure is tricky. That's because the numbers of religious Americans with larger families cancel out statistical heft of secularists with zero-to-two children. Churchgoing Americans have on average five more children. And this is not a small population: sixty percent of Americans say that religion is "very" important to them. (Compare that to, say, France, where it's about ten percent, a good number of whom are soon bound for the church graveyard.) Higher fertility among the faithful keeps our overall numbers stable, even as, in more liberal climes, the population wanes.

Invisibly, fertility in America has emerged as a dividing line in the culture wars. During the 2004 presidential election, fertility rates in states that voted for George W. Bush were twelve percent higher than they were in states that supported John Kerry. County by county, the correlation between family size and political leaning was even stronger. Consider the states with the lowest fertility: New York, Massachusetts, Connecticut, Rhode Island, California, and Vermont. The highest: Arkansas, Oklahoma, Utah, Kentucky, Mississippi, West Virginia. The Red State versus Blue State split that developed under Bush tracks fertility more faithfully than any other measurable factor: on the coasts, we look like Europe, and in between, we look like a prior age.

The Two Americas confront the same dire challenge of parenting without state support. The unchurched do it increasingly by having one child, or none. And the churched do it by depending on the resources provided by their faith community. Thus two systems exist, populated by citizens who subscribe to two radically different philosophies about no less than the meaning of life itself. Some of us map our lives by obedience to a higher power, residing in communities organized to support and perpetuate belief, while others inhabit a less conscripted world of relativism. But this split is relatively new in our history.

The world of smaller families is a "new regime governed by the primacy of individual choice," replacing "a strong normative structure based on a familistic ideology supported by the church and state." So says demographer and social theorist Ron Lesthaeghe, an only child himself and the author of a landmark theory called the Second Demographic Transition. Along with colleague Dirk van de Kaa, Lesthaeghe introduced this concept in 1986 in a Dutch sociology journal. The First Demographic Transition defines a shift away from high birthrates afforded by medical and industrial advances—the move from my grandmother's ten siblings to my mother's two. The first mass reduction in fertility can be understood explicitly in terms of time and money, like the rise in living standards, employment, economic growth, and material values. The second one, however, is born out of a battle of ideas. It is about our minds, our souls, our very redefinition of the meaning of life.

Lesthaeghe contends that our needs changed as civilization advanced and industrialization relegated most subsistence concerns to the past. No longer did we worry about infant mortality, the boll weevil, the violence of weather. Instead, our focus shifted to Abraham Maslow's higher order needs, or what we require when the lower order needs—physical safety, financial security—are met. Individualistic and expressive, these higher order needs essentially add up to self-actualization: creativity, spontaneity, confidence, and achievement.

"The worst of doing one's duty was that it apparently unfitted one for doing anything else," Edith Wharton wrote in *The Age of Innocence,* her 1920 novel that questioned the monomaniacal power of marriage and family. Indeed, the Roaring Twenties threw open the door to questioning such duty and definitions. Rather than pondering duty, the zeitgeist told its denizens to just kick up their heels and *live.* Until the crash of 1929, that is. There tends to be a single assumption explaining why fertility tanked internationally and the number of only children spiked in the decade that followed. The common belief holds that parents chose to radically limit family size because of economics. Certainly the Great Depression was a sinkhole that pulled the industrialized world into its depths—and we know that when the stock market falls, so do the numbers of babies delivered. This was surely the case when income dropped anywhere from fifteen to fifty-eight percent for families from 1929 to 1933, which includes the gains for women heading off to work for the first time during those years.

But the Second Demographic Transition explains the rise of singletons and the child-free-by-choicers not just as an economic response, but a philosophical one. It's the result of widespread secularism, education, and liberalism—the pursuit of personal freedom as a life purpose. Today, says Lesthaeghe, the motivation of low fertility is to achieve greater fulfillment in adulthood, as a parent or not, which emerged as "the expression of secular and anti-authoritarian sentiments of better-educated men and women who held an egalitarian world view," he writes.

As several demographers have asserted—such as Jan Van Bavel in *Population Studies*—the economic crisis was only part of the rise of only children during the Depression. Modernity was the cause as surely as money. The threadbare 1930s emerged from the decadent 1920s, after all. Pleasure-seeking had become a pastime, when people could afford it, and self-actualization a new priority. The Age of Innocence was over, and the breadlines weren't about to bring it back. The loveless marriage (I'm looking at you, Newland Archer) was increasingly spurned. Gender roles began to shift, and with them, the cost of children began to mount. In the United States and abroad, women began to work outside the home, raising the opportunity costs of remaining homebound. Religious identification declined, and with it, the notion of absolute familial duty.

Despite the entirely rational basis for stopping at one— whether it was *we can't afford more* or *we don't want more*—the sudden vanguard of single-child families were treated with suspicion, as a piteous temporary aberration. This, as you may recall from the emerging stereotype of the selfish parent, was the era in which mothers of one child were called "deliberate malingerers" lacking the "pioneer courage" to suck it up and breed again for the good of society. A collective disdain emerged both for working mothers and for families looking for state relief. In his vast California-based study of Depression-era families, Glen Elder quoted subjects who feel that "something is wrong with a man who can't support his family," even in such dire times. Women should be staying home, making babies and caring for them, and "providing examples of the family as an adaptive resource in times of economic trouble," no matter the cost, wrote Elder. And so, despite the new prevalence of the single-child family, the notion of two types of families—normal ones with both a Dick *and* a Jane, and abnormal ones with a miserable only child—remained unchallenged.

Twenty years later the postwar baby boom reversed this fertility decline and locked the windows against the winds of radicalism that had gathered into a global threat. But in spite of a new breed of conservatism, we continued a march toward familial transformation. Divorce, the vanguard of the fifties, stood in legal and cultural defiance of the strict morality of the church that had been enforced by the state. On its heels came the Pill, legal abortion, the mass sanctioning of nonprocreative sex. It took less than a century to reverse the millennia-old definitions of what a woman was, what a mother was, what a life was. For a spell, Anne Roiphe and T. Berry Brazelton delivered verbal fist bumps to any woman who would stand her ground and stop at one if she wanted to. It was the age in which Helen Reddy's "I Am Woman" reached the top of the Billboard chart, and feminist author Susan Brownmiller became *Time* magazine's Woman of the Year. By the midseventies total fertility in America sank to the 1.8 mark and remained there well into the eighties.

But then came the backlash. After the Equal Rights Amendment failed in Washington and the Christian Coalition began to strengthen, the traditional mother-of-two-or-more became deified once more. Women who joined the swiftly growing numbers of deeply faithful began to have more children. Those who remained secular filled that space with other pursuits—to foment their wanderlust and intellectual curiosity, enroll in graduate programs, and seek fulfilling romance. This Maslovian drift, as Lesthaeghe calls it, is "now reaching saturation," in secular American and non-Muslim Europe. Over the past half century nonreligious Americans have rejected the rectitude of Church and State, with strict concepts of family at the top of the list. But the faithful among us have run in the other direction, entrenched in antique notions of the family as the cornerstone of God and Country.

Lesthaeghe has found that what he calls Second Demographic Transition variables—namely, the postponement of marriage and parenting, and support of gay coupling and abortion rights—have become the single best predictor of a person's politics in this country. This correlation extends far beyond voting habits by income and education levels. It was Lesthaeghe's 2009 study published in *Population and Development Review* that drew the lines of Red State–Blue State America in terms of family size. Why we have money, industry, democracy, and still more babies than any other developed nation has long been understood as the exceptionalism of American fertility. Lesthaeghe believes this should be recast as "bipolarity." "What makes the United States particularly interesting in the overall Western context," he says, "is that the conservative and religious right is openly and vocally trying to fight back against the values of the Second Demographic Transition," organizing against Planned Parenthood, forcing the closure of abortion clinics, attempting to outlaw choice, and now demonizing contraception. As he points out, nothing like this has happened in Europe, Canada, or Australia.

In the United States, our bipolarity only underscores our exceptionalism. Other than a single outlier, says Charles Westoff, a Princeton demographer who has devoted much of his career to understanding the relationship between faith and fertility, "As rich societies become more secular, the status of women changes, women's options in life increase, the value of the individual rises, fertility and population growth decline." Americans are that out-lier, "fecund to none," as Ben Wattenberg wrote in his book *Fewer*.

And so while fertility continued to fall in Europe, it made a steady climb back up to replacement rates in the United States— to thirty-four percent higher than on the continent. The EU gave their low-breeding citizens free day care. We gave the Duggars and their then-seventeen children a television show. And so we have one America with the values and birthrates of the developed world, and another with the values and birthrates of a society we evolved beyond generations ago. Unfortunately, both Americas have the same family policy.

Highway 76 slashes through Branson, a tiny town in the Ozarks, made famous for the neon-lit theaters that line the asphalt, where gospel and doo-wop covers are performed daily for the tourists who make it the number-one bus destination in America. Most of the acts appearing here specialize in God-loving Americana under red, white, and blue lights. Vocalists belt out inspirational hits in front of giant video screens with pixels of gloriously wav-ing American flags and cowboys kneeling beside their horses. A striking number of the performers are supersized family acts. They rib each other as good-natured siblings do, alternat-ing Motown singalongs with country anthems about sitting on Daddy's knee, watching the fireflies. During the intermission for the eight-sibling act The Haygoods, I eavesdrop on an audience member approaching their father and manager, all big gold eye-glass frames in a cloud of hair spray. "How did you afford music lessons for all of those beautiful children?" she asks, astonished. "We didn't—the Lord provides it," he replies reverently. She covers her heart with her hand and blinks back tears of wonder.

Of course, no one dabs their eyes with a red, white, and blue handkerchief when they hear stories more like mine. *You settled in New York, became a writer, married a photographer, refused to give up on your own ambitions, lived life according to your own terms and pleasures, and became a mother? How did you do it?* I often find myself thinking of a *Sex in the City* episode when single Carrie Bradshaw ruefully reflects upon all the baby showers, children's birthday parties, and weddings she's attended, all the presents she's been obligated to purchase and the energy she's been expected to devote to congratulating people moving through the traditional life course. These are the narrative moments we lionize, always fawning over the next baby, and necessarily so, since it's not like one can celebrate a nonevent like the choice not to reproduce.

The badge of pioneer courage pinned upon the choices that lead to fecundity is hardly a century-old aberration. In a 2011 GOP debate, candidates breathlessly competed over whose family was biggest, from Mitt Romney's five children, to Rick Santorum's seven, to the twenty-three foster children Michelle Bachmann raised. Ron Paul even tried to best them all by counting the number of babies he delivered as an obstetrician. The game was to see who could win at being most American—American meaning *family*. Big families are praised from the pulpit, the podium, and throughout popular culture. Meanwhile, the implication crouches silently: there are two family stories, one patriotic and venerable, the other selfish and suspect.

Demographer Philip Morgan has been keeping his eye on the tight grip that faith tends to have on American fertility. "We learn desires," he says. "We tend to tell stories that are culturally acceptable to justify our behavior." One story can explain quite clearly why religious people intend to have more children and then follow through on those intentions. That story can be understood as simply as following the Biblical mandate of Genesis 1:28, *Be fruitful and multiply.*

Off a rural road outside Columbia, Missouri, Steve and Karma are raising their five kids, one recently adopted. Their children aren't allowed to use the Internet (a source of constant dispute), and can't even watch movies their Christian friends show at sleepovers. But Karma, an emergency room nurse, says, "Sure, it says to be fruitful and multiply, but you have to take it into context of what God is asking you to do." She rolls her eyes at the notion of another kid. Still, for two months they prayed over whether to adopt Caroline and they felt led by God to do so. They had recently added two bedrooms to their three-bedroom house, and there was room on the enormous round sectional in the great room for another pair of legs in Christian school sweatpants (they homeschool half time), but the expense was still great. As Phillip Longman, author of *The Empty Cradle,* tells me, "It really isn't economically rational to have kids. So who does? People who are not economically rational. There has to be a force telling them to do it, in their head."

"We trust that each time we have another kid, God will make sure we get what we need," Steve, an accountant, says. Indeed, it was their church that provided the hand-me-downs, the babysitting help, the encouragement. "Our church is our family network," says Steve. "If I didn't have my faith, this wouldn't be my focus.

Church and family, that's what my life revolves around." I have spent more than a decade in and out of Evangelical communities—as a journalist—and have heard this sentiment expressed more times than I can count.

But there was a time, not too long ago, when even among the believers family life didn't require this level of immersion in the church. Instead of calling on a community of believers to be a family network, people used to have an actual family network. Three generations gathering on the portico, in the kitchen, around the table—and everyone's porticoes, kitchens, and tables an easy stroll away. Family was the type of help you now have to hire. Unless, like Karma and Steve, you have a church to provide you with babysitting shares, potlucks, hand-me-downs, and freezers full of casseroles labeled with other women's handwriting. Why would anyone agitate for different family policy when you have all you need in a tight self-selecting—and self-reinforcing—community?

This is the culture not just for Evangelicals, but for a huge portion of America's Hispanic population, where only children are an anomaly. In fact, while our total fertility may hover just above 2.1, when you subtract Latina mothers, that number sinks down to 1.7. In Austin, the biggest diocese in the big state of Texas, some churches are adding eight hundred Hispanic students a year to Sunday school. In sessions required in preparation for marriage and catechism, deacons strictly teach natural family planning; the state of Texas waives its marriage license fee for taking the class. "We're seeing the population just exploding here. Four children is the new two," says Christian Gonzales, who heads up Communications for the Diocese of Austin. "People aren't postponing kids here like they are elsewhere for college or career. After high school it's time to get married and have kids," he tells me. Nearby, at the Dolores Parish church, grandmother Raquel, all ample bosom and crimson fingernails, gathers her family every Sunday. Of her nine children, all have become parents. "When I go to sleep at night, I bless everyone's beds," she says. "It takes a good twenty minutes." She tells me that she believes, as her mother taught her and as she has tried to impart to her own children, that the bigger the family, the happier the family. When I tell her I'm an only child, she clucks and shakes her head.

Brad Wilcox, who heads up the National Marriage Project, agrees with her. At age forty, he's already a father of eight. Wilcox recently presented his own findings that challenge the research that families are happiest with one child. He learned that family happiness falls on a curvilinear graph, where none or one may rank high, but so do families with five or more children. "That fathers and mothers of large families are partly happier because they find more meaning in life, receive more support from friends who share their faith, and have a stronger religious faith than their peers with smaller families," he says. His recent National Marriage Project survey found that parents in big families are twice as likely to attend regular services as parents with small families. "Religious men and women feel called by God or encouraged by their religious networks of friends and family members to have large families," he explained in the report.

Without that faith, his graphs tell us, bigger families actually aren't happier at all. Imagine what Steve and Karma's family would look like without the help their church has given each of the five times they've brought a new child into their increasingly crowded home. They can't. "Yeah, right! It would be impossible," says Karma. In the United States, religious institutions and their communities play a similar role to the family care–providing state in Europe. If you're a believer, there's a good chance you can make that work for you. But what if you're not? Without faith "in God and family," as is so often intoned in this country, you're simply flying solo.

It's easy to see how raising an only child within a church community has become an exceptional act, and a daunting one. Joanne, a devout makeup artist in Parsippany, New Jersey, knows this too well. After she had Ruth thirteen years ago, she simply could not reconcile having a second child. "It was really hard," she tells me. "I made myself feel bad. Sure, they were my own insecurities, but you know, you spend your whole life hearing and believing, 'The more kids, the more glory to God.'" Over the years Joanne came to the understanding, she says, that "it was God's purpose for me to have one so I could reach out to others."

In church communities, this defense is a common one: choosing to stop at one as a manifestation of what many Christians call "God's perfect plan." An Evangelical mother named Leslie in Amarillo, Texas, says her ten-year-old son, Bryar, is the one "God meant for us to have and the only one we want." It took Leslie years to conceive, which has underscored Bryar's chosen nature. But she's also completely sanguine about how she can't imagine being able to afford another. Bryar plays four sports, and "It's already expensive," says Leslie. "Forget college, insurance, and a car. Imagine if we were running around to twice as many sporting events, buying twice as many uniforms and tennis shoes," she tells me. "People around here think we're crazy. But to tell you the truth, if by some weird twist I got pregnant accidentally, we would be devastated." Of course, for Leslie, at least theoretically and certainly publicly, abortion would not be an option.

—

"You realize," my mother comments one afternoon while we're cooking in her kitchen, "what you're really saying when you're considering committing to an only child."

"What do you mean?" I ask, puzzled.

"You're talking about forming your own personal abortion policy. You're talking about what it means to have an only child if you're pregnant with another."

She's right. But I had never thought about it in quite those terms before. Just as you can be pro-choice and have several kids—and many people are—you can be antiabortion and be adamant you only want one child. But that calculus escalates to a true conflict only if you find yourself accidentally pregnant with another child. At that point you have to decide which is greater: your aversion to terminating a pregnancy or your desire to say that one child is enough.

Certainly, since Dahlia was born, there have been plenty of late periods, yielding plenty of sleepless nights of whispering under the covers with Justin, *what if?*, discussing the possibility of abortion as the sun rises, awaiting the padding of Dahlia's feet announcing her arrival in our bedroom. My own lingering ambivalence about whether to have another child hasn't been tested by that reality—at least not yet. I find myself imagining my mother's own sleepless night, drawing up that pros and cons list, forming her own resolve.

As a mother with a *one and done* approach, only menopause will relieve the anxiety of what it means to become pregnant again by accident. Before I had Dahlia, abortion to me felt like a difficult choice, and one I've had the good fortune never to confront. But it resided in a theoretical realm, one of ethics, one of imaginary roads not taken. Only since I've witnessed what that bundle of cells can become, not just as a theoretical child, but the one whose nose I kiss and whose development fascinates me constantly, do I have a relationship with what my own abortion might truly mean. For those of us who either steadfastly choose to stop at one, or struggle with that choice, this poses a real dilemma. Not a dilemma of rights, or a dilemma of universal ethics, but a dilemma that forces the tactile, engrossed love I feel for my daughter into battle with the sound reasoning behind the choice to stop at one.

And I find myself thinking that if I were to choose to terminate as a mother, I'd be stigmatized as a prenatal Medea, exceptional for my decision. Not so. National Abortion Federation president Vicki Saporta tells me that every year since 2008, nearly *three quarters* of the women who've reached out to them looking to terminate a pregnancy are already mothers themselves.

Anne Baker has been counseling St. Louis–area abortion seekers for thirty-five years. (Over the years she has advised more than a few women who had previously protested outside her clinic.) She says the number of mothers coming in has swelled markedly since the economic downturn, and especially since the 1970s recession when she started out. Baker wrote up a list of twenty-five reasons mothers commonly give as to why they feel they can't have another child, acknowledging the fact that there are as many contexts to this choice as there are women who struggle to make it. But far and above—and increasingly—women tell her that they choose to terminate to protect the family they already have. It's an economic choice most of the time. Baker has also noted a growing sector of women like myself who are "less apologetic about it than they used to be about saying they're a good mom and for them to continue to be a good mom, they choose to do it with one."

"The less in control of a woman's life she is, the more the public supports her right to make that choice," former Planned Parenthood president Gloria Feldt tells me. "The more she is in control of her life, saying this is the life I choose, the less people support it." But nobody seems surprised that there's a big increase in abortion rates five to nine months following job losses. You could argue that choice is being forced by a higher power (a boss, a corporation, a bank account) rather than one's own desire. But someone like myself, who could handle another child if I chose to move to a less expensive zip code and tried to get a job with a more stable paycheck? "It's scandalous for white women like you and me," says Jennifer Baumgardner, who wrote the book *Abortion & Life*. And it matters little on what side of the faith divide you reside.

The choice to have a single child has become even more complicated since in-vitro-fertilization doctors realized that implanting multiple embryos in a patient's womb yielded a better success rate. The likelihood of becoming pregnant with multiples has soared and raised a new dilemma: whether to have just one after becoming pregnant with two or three. When Ruth Pawdawer wrote about what she termed the "two-minus-one pregnancy" for *The New York Times Magazine*, she reported that doctors advise patients to keep private their decision to reduce to a singleton. As IVF procedures have climbed rapidly in response to increasingly common delayed fertility, selective reduction is still rare, but it's on the rise.

Amy Richards is someone who did not take the advice to keep her decision private. She published a personal account in that same publication about her choice to terminate two of her three triplets. Richards lived in a five-floor walk-up, was fairly broke, and entirely committed to her developing career as a writer and activist. An only child herself, she is a cofounder of the Third Wave Foundation, and a vocal proponent of abortion rights. The choice made perfect sense to her to have only one child (at that time; she's since had another) when pregnant with three. But don't underestimate how much will it required.

In Seattle, a woman named Ariel, a fourth-generation only child, made a very different choice from Richards when faced with the question of multiples, but one just as rooted in resolve. Ariel is also pro-choice, but she never wanted to wrestle with the selective reduction, despite the fact that she was completely committed to having an only child. When she had a hard time conceiving and started the IVF process, she made a hard choice. She asked her doctor to implant not two embryos, as is the typical procedure, but just one. "Listen, IVF is awful. God bless it for existing, but it's a terrible experience," she tells me. "I was willing to risk it to be sure that if it worked, it only worked once. I wasn't going to have two kids, and I didn't want to have to make the choice not to once it already happened." It worked. And if it hadn't, she was prepared to go through it with just one embryo over and over again until it did.

Her strategy may have been unique, but Ariel's staunchness to stop at one is not uncommon among only children. Remember all that intensity, all that participation in a tiny society free of diversity and often brimming with family dogma? It follows that only children are likely to repeat their parents' choices, especially when it comes to family size. In 1981 Denise Polit published a paper on the life choices of adult singletons. Their fertility intentions, she found, tended toward having only children themselves. (Furthermore, the female onlies were far less likely to think that it was her husband's choice to decide whether she should work or not, or how many children she should have.) And Polit discovered that only *four percent* of singletons fall into the category of people who say that religion has a very important role in their lives. "It is the unique quality of being an only," she writes, "which contributes to smaller family size goals, and greater secularism."

In other words, those of us who are more Second Demographic–minded tend to come from small families and do whatever it takes to limit our own family size. You can see why some thinkers predict we're unbreeding ourselves into oblivion.

The numbers are as good as prophecy to Eric Kaufmann, author of *Shall the Religious Inherit the Earth?* Low fertility among less religious liberals and high fertility among conservative believers will result in the end of secularism. The more people inherit patriarchal, family-expanding faiths, the more they will determine the character of the world. Kaufmann predicts the ongoing culture wars, globally and in the United States, will be won not through the verbal battles of preaching or politics but through a competition of cradles. As he tells me, "Demography shapes these big cultural questions. It operates like compound interest."

Ladies and gentlemen of a certain stripe, prepare to be outbred. It won't happen tomorrow. But according to his projections, generations will look back at this thing called secular liberalism and consign it to the slag heap of Zoroastrianism and Manichaeanism. He points out that this isn't the first time we've seen demography reshape the world's beliefs: a tiny minority of the followers of Jesus Christ exhibited disproportionately high fertility for centuries until their fringe movement became the majority faith of the West. As Walter Russell Mead wrote in *National Interest*, native Europe appears to have "lost the biological will to live." British theologian David Hart has noted, albeit dramatically, it's "fairly obvious that there is some direct, indissoluble bond between faith and the will to a future," as expressed in the production of heirs to carry on a familial—and religious—legacy.

"Your Evangelicals and Hispanics are our Muslims," Ron Lesthaghe chuckles to me over coffee, "and all of us freethinkers have suicidal demography." In truth, the Bible and the Koran are both pronatal texts. Just as pastors invoke Genesis 1:28 with abandon, so even the Turkish prime minister has told his minions to have more babies because "Allah wants it," adding that contraception is "treason." While conservative Christian and Hispanic Catholic fertility may be significant in the States, in Europe, the influx and high fertility of Muslims has become a topic of great debate and, for some, anxiety. Pew Research Center's Forum on Religion & Public Life recently published a report on the global Muslim population that projected their growth in Europe at almost one third over the next twenty years alone, from 44.1 million to 58.2 million, approaching double digit percentages of the overall population in several countries.

Kaufmann says that this high fertility is linked with religious orthodoxy. He's found that women committed to sharia have on average twice as many children as Muslim women who don't live by Islamic law. Yet while those numbers represent significant averages, they are simply that: averages. The Muslim world is nothing if not diverse, and that's as true of fertility as anything else. In Niger, for example, women have an average of more than seven kids; in Bosnia that number hovers around one. (Just compare the childlessness of Sarajevo, which is being treated like an epidemic, with the late Osama bin Laden's twenty-seven children and his father's fifty-three.)

They don't come more provocative than Longman, who wrote in *The Empty Cradle* that "the future will belong to those who reject markets, reject learning, reject modernity, and reject freedom." Longman hardly minces words when I ask what he thinks of Kaufmann's projections and the notion that our certain future is a world of religious conservatism dictated by who makes the most babies. "The majority of people in modern society are thoroughly secular and breeding below replacement rates, and it's a road to extinction," he tells me. "It turns out that the disparity is huge, getting bigger, unprecedented," and, going a step further than Kaufmann, adds, "The influence on the next generation is overwhelming." This means no less, he wrote in a *USA Today* op-ed, than "as the death of the Enlightenment."

Ron Lesthaeghe believes that those dogmatic systems can't help but weaken over time. Unlike Kaufmann's view of a world inhabited by Islamists, Hasidim, and fundamentalist Christians and Catholics, he believes that through immigration, education, and the ever-charging locomotive of modernity, secular liberalism will survive through what he calls "the mental migration of the religious," and that while we'll never see an end to religion as the Enlightenment predicted, it won't be an End of Days for the dogma averse, at least not completely. But he admits that the math doesn't lie: the literal odds are in the favor of the fertile, and the most fertile are the most faithful. It's as simple as that.

"Should my desire to defend Enlightenment values and a secular future for my kid lead me to have another one?" I ask him.

He grins at me and laughs. "That's adorable," he says. Of course, none of us secularists breed to change the world. We'd need faith to do that.

NINE

TEA LEAVES

n her lifetime, Dahlia will be responsible for 3.1 million pounds of CO_2, twenty-three million pounds of water waste, and more than seven thousand pounds of food waste. Imagine if there were two of her. Or three.

Each day the world expands by the population of Toronto. Our global numbers are expected to increase by 2.5 billion to 9.2 billion by 2050. As economist Jeffrey Sachs calmly wrote in his book *Common Wealth*, that's "too many people to absorb safely." This explosion is mainly relegated to the developing world, where natural resources and food availability are disappearing. But in wealthier places like the United States and the EU, our less-extreme but already vast numbers play just as big a role in hastening the earth's demise.

The richest countries, with twenty percent of the global population, account for eighty-six percent of the world's total private consumption. A single child today in an industrialized nation will add more to consumption and pollution than thirty to fifty children born in developing ones. Each baby born in the United States today will add about three hundred times more carbon dioxide to the earth's atmosphere than every baby born in Ethiopia. And so, we have a crisis. It's a crisis of numbers, a crisis of people, a crisis of the rich world and the poor world, the developed countries and the quickly developing ones.

I am hardly a Greenpeace activist. When I was given the opportunity to buy a hybrid car, I opted for a Jeep. I often forget to bring my own bag to the grocery store. I hate the fluorescent bulbs my husband screwed into all of our light sockets. I love to eat meat. But when I feel guilty, I think of what British environmentalist David Nicholson-Lord told me: "Having fewer kids is the biggest, quickest, cheapest, easiest thing anyone can do to ease the human strain on the planet." What if a larger family were to live by a code that restricts their impact as much as possible? Nicholson-Lord just laughs at my question. "There's no such thing as zero impact. There's not even such a thing as close-to-zero impact. That's reality. Fewer kids equal less impact, period," he says. A person who is not born consumes nothing, wreaks no havoc on the earth, has no possible footprint.

And yet writers like Ben Wattenberg, a senior fellow at the American Enterprise Institute, contend that there is a moral failing in the choice to curb family size. "Is it irresponsible for the species to breed itself downward? Human life has a purpose. Human beings may choose not to have children, or to have only one child, but the human species does not have that choice," he wrote in his book *Fewer*. Don't believe the United Nations fertility projections, he says, nor the "religious" dogma of the greens. Just as we should be worried about finance, not feminism, in his view, we should worry about the economy, not the environment.

But even more shocking to me than Wattenberg's argument that humans have no right to limit their family size is the fact that to most *environmentalists,* it's near blasphemy to speak of curbing our numbers. As Alan Weisman, author of *The World Without Us,* tells me about overpopulation: "They refer to this as the third rail of environmentalism." A simple glance at the issues pages of any major environmental website lays bare the absence of concern about the number of consuming and polluting humans on earth. Pick up any greening guide in your local bookstore, such as *50 Simple Steps You Can Take to Save the Earth* or *How to Reduce Your Carbon Footprint.* Printed on all those departed trees is nary a suggestion that perhaps we should have fewer babies. We're still debating paper or plastic, rather than people.

It's a thorny issue. The green movement has done a great job gaining influence via the notion that small, consumer-centered steps can save the planet. Don't you feel virtuous when you remember to bring the damn bags to the grocery store? (I know I do.) As David Nicholson-Lord tells me, the green effort is "increasingly wary of inducing guilt and negative feelings among its potential audience by warning them of 'problems.' In a sense, it's fallen victim to the feel-good factor. If messages aren't positive and upbeat, people simply stop listening and look the other way."

Pitching the dangers of overpopulation is hardly a winning marketing campaign. "For environmentalists, focusing on overpopulation is a lose-lose-lose proposition. Since it flies in the face of no limits, it is deeply unpopular and gets them accused of being gloomy," Kevin DeLuca, who wrote a book called *Image Politics: The New Rhetoric of Environmental Activism,* tells me. "Overpopulation, like many environmental problems, unfolds slowly and without the requisite dramatic visuals. How do we illustrate the overpopulation problem—pictures of cute babies?"

Discussing an environmental population crisis conjures notions of colonialists and eugenicists, state control of our bodies, and erosion of our personal liberties and biological birthright. Moreover, economists, historians, and scientists debate if consumption, as it relates to the population swell, is the true villain, or if technology will develop to solve our apocalyptic woes, or if an economic boost will save the day. Consumption has overtaken overpopulation as the demon in our midst. It's much easier to quantify and control, with ready-made visual aids.

As Columbia University historian and author of *Fatal Misconception: The Struggle to Control World Population*, Matthew Connelly, tells me, it's not the 1.2 billion consumers in China who are the problem; "it's the three hundred million aspiring to have lives like Americans have" who contribute thirty percent of the world's fossil fuels. I am certainly not discounting China's lax environmental laws—despite the One Child Policy, I know firsthand how much harder it is to breathe in Chinese cities than it was even five years ago, and I haven't even visited factory towns.

I reflect on the seventy new toys the average American child receives each year, most of which are made in those Chinese factory towns. And then I look into my own paper bags, shudder at my own consumption, and wonder if even one child was a personal luxury for which the green movement should have clucked its silent tongue. These days Greenpeace never discusses overpopulation, despite the fact that the human race has expanded by fifty percent since the issue was in vogue. As a public information officer at Greenpeace says when I ask for comment, "We don't really have anyone primed to talk about overpopulation. I don't know if we historically even had a position on it."

Today's population blindness among so many environmentalists would have shocked activists in the patchouli-scented seventies, when a group called Zero Population Growth was first organized. As anxiety about what was perceived as population control slowly spread through the culture, the group changed its name to the rather neutral moniker of Population Concern. But even this name proved too loaded, and in 2003 they scrubbed out any sense of their purpose and called themselves Interact Worldwide. Paul Ehrlich, the original organization's founder, has as much to do with population's pariah status as anyone. His prediction, which sets off page one of his 1968 bestseller *The Population Bomb*, is as follows: "In the 1970s the world will undergo famines—hundreds of millions of people are going to starve . . ." Instead, people had more to eat than ever before.

Ehrlich's doomsaying was accompanied by a massive backlash against the subject as the seventies ticked by and the bomb didn't. Famines were diverted by the so-called green revolution, a series of agricultural research and development initiatives that coaxed untold stores of food from the land, which then led to our current population spike and food crisis—"the population of the species tends to rise to meet the available food supply," Alan Weisman points out forty years later. "Instead of solving hunger on earth, all we did was produce four to five times the number of hungry people," destroying our soil and disrupting our ecology in doing so. Plus, the debate over population rates unfailingly comingles with the concept of eugenics (Who has the right to breed?). Which certainly can feel just as threatening today, when you think about all those academics in Europe—those demographers who began their careers helping the subequatorial world to have fewer babies—shifting their research to convince the citizens of the north to have more. Our smaller, paler families often consume at ten times the rate of larger, darker ones—and yet it's their fertility we want curbed and ours we want increased.

Justine, who was born in the early seventies to two Australian environmental journalists, knows that according to her family her lack of siblings was a clearly articulated choice based on the planet's welfare, rather than their own. "My mom and my dad thought it was unethical to bring more than one child into the world when the environment was so endangered by people," she tells me. "But I think that was all bullshit. I think she used that as an excuse. If she really cared that much, she would have had more of us so we could have helped to protect the earth."

Her mom was afraid to own up to her desires, Justine says, and so she cloaked them in progressive dogma. "She was worried she wouldn't have the time to work, to live her own life. Sure, now my life is my kids, but I know the two of them will be raised to make a difference to the planet. I honestly think I'm doing more for the earth with my two," she says. "The problem isn't the size of our population, it's what it's doing."

Justine's kids—and she's now pregnant with a third—will likely grow up to be engaged citizens, unless they truly rebel from their parents' own behavior modeling. But the oceans couldn't care less. Each one of her children, and mine, as long as they enjoy heat, air conditioning, and vehicular commuting, will be responsible for the annual emissions of 620 round-trip flights between London and New York, according to the Optimum Population Trust, which in 2011 changed its name to Population Matters.

And, yes, the numbers in terms of global population may not be as sinister en masse as they were in the early seventies when Justine's parents made their choice, but as long as these children aren't raised in a developing country, that hardly matters.

The fatal electric charge of the "third rail" is not so much acknowledging our teeming future, but discussing what should be done about it. Perhaps nobody understands this better than Al Gore. In the documentary *An Inconvenient Truth,* Gore mentions that our overpopulation is the leading factor of climate change, backing up his claim with soaring graphs of overpopulation in developing countries. But when, under the closing credits, the film offers solutions for change, we are told to buy a hybrid car and better lightbulbs. But lay off the layettes? Critics of Gore's film eagerly lambasted him for flying all over the world to share his urgent message, but I've yet to find a critique of his four-child family's aggregate carbon footprint.

It's as though we've all agreed that the sanctity of the family is irreproachable. We venerate the personal choice to reproduce, the desire to make all those cute babies (as long as they aren't in those overpopulous countries) regardless of the literally unthinkable cost. What on earth is more purely, viscerally, ecstatically optimistic than a new life, especially a life born into love? Even I, reluctant initially to join the maternal ranks, can resoundingly answer that rhetorical question. When Al Gore gazes upon his many grandchildren, I doubt the very first thing he imagines is his chart on American fossil-fuel consumption.

There's one figure you won't see in his film, or on the Greenpeace website, or on the side of your organic milk carton. In researching *The World Without Us,* Alan Weisman called upon Sergei Scherbov, the research group leader at the Vienna Institute of Demography, to run the numbers: What would happen if, starting right now, everyone made the choice to have only one child? Scherbov ascertained that within one hundred years our population would shrink to 1.6 billion, less than one-third of today's human race. Those smaller numbers would radically curb the erosion of our natural resources.

Maybe One is essentially a booklength consideration of many of these ideas and more (using different, older data—the book was published in 1999), written by Bill McKibben. He starts off in unteachable eagle territory, in G. Stanley Hall's archives, and puts Hall's erroneous allegations of singletons to the Toni Falbo test. On the shoulders of his conclusion that only children turn out just fine—sometimes even better—than kids with siblings, McKibben builds the environmental case for stopping at one. He ends the book describing driving home from the urologist's office with a bag of ice between his legs. His solution, after having a child, was to get a vasectomy.

There's a lot worth quoting in *Maybe One*, but I'll leave you to discover it for yourself, if you're interested. I will, however, share an aspect of his conviction that particularly resonates with me. After itemizing some of the challenges facing us on this planet, and in the societies scattered over its surface, McKibben imagines *"the energy freed by having smaller families may be some of the energy needed to take on these next challenges* [his italics], to *really* take them on, not just to announce that they're important, or to send a check, or to read an article, but to make them central to our lives." And then he adds, "The Church should not find that argument so foreign. Priests are celibate, at least in part, because it allows them to make Christ their bride, to devote all their energies to the other tasks set before us on earth." Perhaps if this argument could be softened and applied to all of God's children, and not just the clergy, our national liberal-conservative bipolarity could be somewhat rectified, our two Americas knit together as something closer to one.

Resource dilution extends to far more than what children gain from their parents. When our personal resources are stretched thin, not just as parents but as people, we lose the space to ruminate upon what confronts our lives, our societies, and our planet, much less to participate in meaningful change. We can hardly find the energy to address our personal challenges, not to mention our global ones. "Who's got the time?" we commiserate with each other. Of course, it's not just our personal resources we're diluting, it's our planet's, as we fill bigger shopping carts in bigger box stores and drive bigger cars home to bigger houses in service of our families. We're too consumed by the business of daily living to realize what burdens we're really carrying. This is the behavior we teach our children, who will determine the fate of the next generation's personal, economic, and ecological resources—finite, all. Instead of demonstrating a commitment to the world we inhabit, we model what it means to have nothing left to give.

On Facebook, a friend—a mother of an only child named Ivan—posts the following status update: "So, the feminist foremothers were right that you can work, be a great mom and even have sex. And be politically active too! But they didn't anticipate that we would try to add two more things into the mix: volunteering at our kids' public schools AND engaging in all sorts of earth-saving domestic activities. This, it turns out, is a stretch. The worms in my compost have just died. Ivan blames me for being inattentive to them. He is right." A flutter of forty comments immediately appear, most of which reveal how uptight we've become about our ecology and our domestic responsibility; they mainly write to express concern for Ivan, or the worms. ("I'm only mildly troubled by the worms," she feels compelled to clarify in her own comment; "I thought it was a funny parable about the contemporary female condition.")

It's madness enough when there's only *one* Ivan—plus worms and school volunteerism—to manage. Now multiply that madness times two or three and see how all that work and terrific parenting and great sex and political action adds up. It probably doesn't, which means it's time to subtract something. There's simply no choice. My guess is most of us, looking at that list, would reduce by necessity. Civic engagement goes first. Then sex. Then work. Then parenting—parenting is always unavoidably last on this list. "Our obsession with parenting is an avoidance strategy. It allows us to substitute our own small world for the world as a whole," Erica Jong wrote in *The Wall Street Journal*. "If you are busy raising children without societal help and trying to earn a living during a recession, you don't have much time to question and change the world that you and your children inhabit."

The more children we have, the more we speed up the earth's destruction; the more time we spend parenting to the exclusion of all else, the more we close ourselves off to that reality. It's a treadmill: we're exhausting our personal resources in tandem with our natural resources. Within the chattering classes, parents use their advanced degrees to power play-date discussions over cloth diapers or recycled ones or worry over the worms in the compost as they add another child, and then another, to help devour the planet. It's a status game of righteousness: which family can be

most consumed with conscientiousness, which parents can mar-
tyr themselves on a pyre of sustainably sourced logs. There's nothing wrong with compost and cupcakes, as long as you can keep
one eye trained on the future of the larger world, and that's not
an easy thing to do. Instead, so many greener-than-thou parents,
quite literally failing to see the plundered forests for the trees
when considering the environmental costs of our families, debate
the righteousness of what we consume, and not how many of us
are consuming it.

CONCLUSION

AGAINST FOLLY

t's a little after six in the morning, and we're in the dining room, drinking coffee and watching Dahlia improvise some ballet moves to a Flaming Lips song. The cost of my birth control has just doubled, and I'm complaining about the financial and bodily expense I've had to endure over my reproductive years, expressing bitterness about years of burden bearing still to come. Justin blurts out, "Maybe I should have a vasectomy." When Bill McKibben wrote about his, I developed a full-blown crush. Turns out when my husband volunteers to get snipped, I burst into tears, run up to our bedroom, and throw myself onto the pillows like a heartsick teenager. My tears don't subside until Justin has come home from carrying Dahlia all the way to school on his shoulders. Despite all the rational information that supports my reluctance to have another kid, all the research demonstrating that only children are fine, all the data suggesting the additional sacrifices another kid would require, making the choice not to have another child is still fraught with conflict. It's an emotional struggle that, it turns out, no set of numbers and analysis can erase.

John Hodgman, the comic writer, wrote an essay for the book *Only Child: Writers on the Singular Joys and Solitary Sorrows of Growing Up Solo* called "Apologia to My Second Child." The essay is his explanation for choosing not to give his daughter the advantages of an only childhood, like he had. "I trust you shall never quite forgive us for this," he wrote. After his mother's death, and after the terror of one September morning when he feared his wife would never emerge from a burning tangle of steel in lower Manhattan, he realized that in a family of three, the "triangle [can] suddenly collapse, and what is left when it does is nothing at all." And so, he explains to his second child, he feels he needs another to mitigate his looming "absolute awful heartache." But more than the fear of that heartache, this is why I cried this morning: Hodgman wrote to his yet-unborn son, and, indirectly, to his existing daughter that as a sibling, "you will be freer to fail." That's a freedom I have never known, which I may never be able to give Dahlia if she remains my one and only.

On some level, surely Hodgman and I are both buying into a fantasy of how liberating siblings would be, eradicating pressure and existential fears by dint of their mere birth. Justin doesn't feel free to fail, though he has a younger sister. In fact, I don't know anyone who does. We all construct stories to explain ourselves, and in doing so we highlight some elements of what made us, and discard others. Never getting kissed in high school, getting pregnant, being the fat kid, being dyslexic, being gay, having a wicked older sibling, having no siblings at all—we latch on to single narratives to define ourselves to ourselves and others.

These narratives are often anchored in the characters we make of mothers and fathers. Sometimes the stories are ones in which our parents are the protagonists in their own lives: divorce, an affair, dreams perennially deferred, resentments calcified into unhappy homes. Sometimes it's about our parents' relationship to us: they were too religious, they were too radical, they were too discipline minded, they were too lenient, they were consumed with themselves, they were consumed with us. Parenting used to be just one part of adulthood. Today it is considered nearly all that matters. And so parents compromise their own freedom, and in doing so, they compromise their children's.

Two-and-a-half was when it started, I remember. Almost every woman I knew who had been pregnant when I was, suddenly was pregnant again. So I should hardly have been surprised when Dahlia looked up from her dinosaur jigsaw puzzle and said, "Mama, I want a sister."

"Why do you want a sister, love?"

"I want to sing 'Rock-a-bye' to her." Dahlia sang "Rock-a-bye Baby," gazing down lovingly at the imaginary baby she cradled in her arms. "And I want to teach her things."

I felt my heart dissolve. "What else?" I asked.

"I want crackers."

"What do you want more? Crackers or a sister?"

"Crackers. And juice."

I wish I could say that was the end of Dahlia's requests for a sibling. But in truth, such demands are rare, and when she brings it up, she does so with a sidelong glance I call "testing face."

A few studies from the eighties suggested that kids beg for

a sibling when mothers demonstrate anxiety about not having another—if they've tried to conceive and failed, for example, or if a partner has insisted the family not have another despite her own desires for a second. I am reminded of this when talking to Rosa, a mother of a six-year-old girl who sits on her lap pulling on Rosa's shirt, begging *pleasepleaseplease* for another baby in the family. Rosa tells her, "I tried, honey, I tried. I tried so hard. I can't have any more." She looks beyond her daughter to me, pressing her lips together and shaking her head. "I don't know what else to tell her. I just try to explain how much I wanted it too." I want to tell her not to express this to her daughter, not yet, but instead I smile sympathetically. I want Rosa to have had what she wanted. But I also want to tell her what Alice Walker's mother would tell women agonized by their inability to have a child: "If the Lord sets you free, be free indeed."

We all know what life without parenthood feels like, what it means to be free indeed. No wonder people say it's never the right time. But the way they most commonly finish that sentence is *to start having children*. As though once you begin, you have to keep going. Once you have one, the knee-jerk assumption is you'll have to have another, while always remembering that freedom in hindsight. It seems the more of a parent you are, the less you are of anything else.

As it often happens, after Walker had her daughter, her mother offered her quite different, "uncharacteristically bad advice: 'you should have another one soon.'" Such advice, Walker writes, derives from the "misguidance women have collected over millennia to help themselves feel less foolish for having more than one child. This pool is called, desperately, pitiably, 'Women's Wisdom.' In fact it should be called 'Women's Folly.'"

But different women want different things. I think of something Edith Wharton wrote nearly a century prior: "Life is either always a tightrope or a feather bed. Give me the tightrope." I don't want the feather bed, myself. I never did.

My high school friend Sarah is pregnant with twins. She desperately wanted a second child, and she's ending up with a third in the bargain. When I tell my mother Sarah's pregnant again, she chides, "Stand your ground." It sounds like a joke, but it isn't one. I get where she's coming from, and yet it rankles me. Still, I say, "Right?" and laugh, thinking, *Just wait until she hears it's twins.* But what I should be able to say to my mother about Sarah, just as I should learn to say about myself to every sanctimoniously intrusive cashier and demographer and cousin and friend is something quite different. I should be able to say, *It's none of your business.*

It's personal, what's involved in getting in and out of pregnancy. When coworkers ask, "What did you do on your day off?" no one ever says, "I spent the afternoon at Planned Parenthood." Nothing could feel more private than family planning. It's understood that the first trimester of every pregnancy is a fiercely guarded secret. Not one single female friend has ever told me that they have had a tubal ligation, and yet rates of women having the procedure have radically jumped in the past few years—certainly I must know someone who made that choice. This fierce privacy maintains the stigma around all aspects of family planning, from abortions to vasectomies. But the need for that privacy also stems from that stigma, from the intense social judgment surrounding sex and its occasional result.

The problem is, it's also political. Not just the right not to have a child, but what happens to our lives when we do. Our right not to carry every fertilization to term is perennially at risk. We fight that political battle, probably not fiercely enough, but we fight it all the same. What we don't fight for is the right to align child rearing with a meaningful, engaged adulthood, what pastor Rick Warren (and I quote him archly, this widely celebrated preacher of wifely submission) would call a *purpose-driven life*. Or dare I say, even a pleasure-driven one. My purposes are secular: to work hard, to play hard, to think hard, to love hard. They are fluid, constantly shape-shifting into new opportunities that require a lack of restraint to fully size. While my motherhood is fluid as well—sometimes consuming, other times more hands-off—it is my most constant permanent purpose. That is the reality I chose for myself. I'm being a good mother not just when I'm running around the playground or making dinner but also when I'm staring at the ocean or yelling at a newspaper editorial. By thriving as the person I want to be, I'm teaching Dahlia that she can too.

It's hard enough to live life on your own terms in a society that constantly tells women what to do with their bodies and what should occupy their minds; it's at least doubly so within the psychological, financial, and temporal constraints of motherhood. As Ann Crittenden in *The Price of Motherhood* has pithily written, "*motherhood*, as opposed to simply being *female*, is a key source of women's inequality." Increasingly, people have begun to agree with her. Crittenden says, "the fact is, generation after generation of American women has yet to achieve what most college-educated women have said they wanted for more than 100 years: a meaningful career *and* a chance to raise children of their own." Ten years after writing those words, Crittenden admits little has changed. However, she says, habits of mind may be shifting: "This may be a change that's largely in our heads, but that is where all real change begins."

Actually, real change began in the seventies and ground to a halt by the mideighties. That's when Ellen Willis wrote in her essay "Looking for Mr. Good Dad": "the problem is not that women's demands for freedom are rocking the boat," which they surely no longer are, "it's that men have the power to set the terms of their participation in child rearing and women don't. So long as mothers must depend on the 'voluntary commitment' of men who can withdraw it without negotiation at any time, we're in trouble no matter what we do." This isn't just a statement about power, but about the logistics determined by that power. As you've read, thirty years after this essay was published, thirty years that could have seen great progress, the US Census considers child care to be parenting when a mother does it, and an "arrangement" when a father does.

As the singleton rate climbs up the Census charts and previously unthinkable numbers of women are opting out of motherhood entirely, there's no question that while we may not be effecting change with our political power, we are with our own fertility. I am often reminded of a comment Gerda Neyer made to me, that everywhere in the world, anything other than two is a strong opinion. Many of us, it turns out, have strong opinions. But we don't tend to lobby with them.

The intensity we bring to the domestic sphere is inversely related to our absence as advocates in the political one. All those hours spent parenting and working mortgages any availability we might have to think about what alternatives might be, and then to fight for them. Americans like to talk about freedom, but we do very little in the way of conceptualizing what freedom might entail outside the realm of national security. We refuse to scale the Maslovian pyramid, to think about freedom as possibility instead of mere protection.

We complain to our spouses and friends instead of our policy makers. Instead of lobbying for a new system, one that addresses the incompatibility of our work lives and our family lives, we set the alarm an hour early to make cookies for the bake sale before rushing in to the office. Furthermore, this is the behavior we model for our sons and daughters—not to imagine change and work for it, but to simply make it through the exhaustion of another day. Who can step off the treadmill long enough to think through another way, much less devote the time to reviving or redefining a women's movement?

It occurs to me, with pronounced irony, that recently the American women who have successfully organized to achieve legislative reform are perhaps our most domestic bound and conservative ones: mothers who homeschool. When I think of homeschooling families I've interviewed, of mothers who have fashioned themselves as committed political firebrands despite the number of kids they usually have to care for and educate, it's no wonder that their children are the most politically engaged and active I've met. (Of course, they've agitated for legal protection, not funding. It's money that makes the battle for better family policy an eminently bloodier one.)

No doubt, feeling that god is on your side is an energizing force, and it seems few Americans these days can effectively look beyond the walls of home or workplace without it. But another group that has achieved hitherto unimaginable political gains is a thoroughly secular one: the gay rights movement. I can't help but note how this movement is majority (if decreasingly) child free. But perhaps it's not about having the time but wanting to commit it to something larger than yourself. Or even realizing that working toward better policy for families *is* making a commitment to yourself. Since the publication of *Get to Work,* Linda Hirshman has largely abandoned her focus on women's rights, after decades of activism and writing. In her late sixties, heterosexual and married, she shifted her attention to the gay rights movement instead. "Why did I give up on women? It's simple," she tells me. "I wanted to work with people who actually wanted to win."

Then again, like the homeschooling movement that won the right to keep their kids out of the school system, the gay rights movement has focused on the clear task of winning the right to marry. These are simple, clear goals, even if they are hard to achieve. And they don't require anyone's tax dollars. By comparison, realigning the relationship between work and parenthood to address the brokenness of our current system would require deep coffers and multipronged plans. This too may be hard to achieve. But if almost every other industrialized country has managed to mitigate their working citizens' struggle with modern parenting, surely we have the potential as well. Until then, I think I'll keep my family small.

Even if my tax dollars paid for Dahlia's day care and health care, she'd still wake me long before the dawn. There would be the periodic tantrum. I'd have to hire a babysitter or call a friend when Justin and I would make plans for a rare dinner out alone. I'd miss her when I was not with her, and occasionally long for freedom from her when I was. I respect myself as a mother for straining at times against the myriad limitations of a parent's life. Even if radical feminist Shulamith Firestone were drafting our family policy, we'd still pay a price to parent. And I'm happy to.

But as a singleton myself, did I pay a price for my mother's relative freedom? And if I choose to continue to have exclusively nonprocreative sex—or delay the choice to breed again until it's a choice no more—am I mortgaging Dahlia's happiness for my own? These are the questions that underlie this book. My intention in writing it is that we should be able to answer them based on information, not fear. It means we answer them for ourselves, facing up to the mixed bag of tendencies that accompany a life without siblings and jettisoning the stereotypes about singletons (though perhaps by example I've confirmed a few along the way). It also means confronting the realities of how a second kid shapes the life of not just our only children, but our own lives, especially as mothers. And it means heaving off the mantle of guilt that so many of us seem to carry when we delay fertility in search of meaningful engagement—professionally, politically, socially, romantically, and with ourselves.

Isn't that meaningful engagement part of what makes us good parents, and good people? How can we help a child develop an authentic self if we have not done the same? It takes some doing to be who we want to be, whether our fruitfulness comes in the form of larger families, or richer interior lives, or both, for people who apparently can handle more than I can. If I choose to stop at one, that's not a referendum on anyone's choice not to. The whole point is to live the life you want.

It's easier to follow accepted wisdom. It's easier to replicate the past than to go your own way. Should I choose to stop at one myself, perhaps I will merely be replicating my mother's choice. But I'd like to think that it's a choice I will have made with significant investigation, on my own terms—and Justin's—and no one else's, the best I can muster. For all of us, this requires dissecting our desires: poking at their still-beating hearts, investigating inside their stomachs to see what has fed them, getting blood on our hands in the process of probing how they survive. In considering desire, we must consider the stories we tell ourselves, about who we are as only children and the parents of potential only children, who we are as citizens of a family and citizens of the world. What happens if, after investigating such desire, one half of a couple feels that another child is the right choice, and the other half disagrees? That, indeed, is a quandary. But one that is surely better deliberated and reconciled when one's own truth, and not a broad cultural message, is doing the talking.

The rest, honestly, is mindful child rearing. It is for anyone, regardless of how many places we set at the dinner table. To that end I have this to say: to hell with sanctimony. To hell with helicopter parenting. To hell with composting and cupcakes. And if you find yourself raising an only child, there are a few simple things you can do. Provide some diversity in the form of plenty of social opportunities. Keep an eye on your own cocooning habits; breaking out of them will be freeing to you and to your kid. Engage in a much larger world and encourage your child to participate alongside you. Think twice about exurban living. Let go a little. Ask yourself if you lean on your kid as a pawn in your partnership, or as a partner if your partnership has dissolved. But, mainly, don't parent by fear or by guilt. Don't live by fear or by guilt either. I know that's easy to say and hard to do, believe me. But there's great power in behavior modeling. Making a home where parents live life according to their own mores is worth a thousand tiger mothers.

I do believe the nuclear family is a social construct—sometimes a useful one, sometimes one that makes me say pseudo-Marxist things like "social control" at dinner parties. Outside of some dystopian scenario, it's hard to imagine reverting to a society where communities raise children. It's harder still to imagine a future where kids are considered a public responsibility, at least in the United States. Our little asphalt-sided, friend-packed house in Brooklyn feels like a radical departure from how other people live, and it's nothing compared to true communal responsibility for children. But our small effort at a more connected way of living does suggest one of many ways we can further redefine the family.

You have to be hiding pretty deep in your prayer closet not to notice that questions about family are rewriting themselves, at least in certain jurisdictions. My own nuclear family is fast becoming an oddity. Think of all the new narratives we can pick to define ourselves: Married gay parents. Unmarried straight parents. Single parents by choice. Stepfathers, stepmothers, stepbrothers, stepsisters, half brothers, half sisters—who even counts as a singleton anymore? I often think of a friend, engaged to a father of two, who is debating whether to have an only child herself, despite the fact that this child is guaranteed to have two stepsiblings.

Susan Sontag, who stopped at one herself, once wrote that "the only interesting answers are those that destroy the questions." I think of this one evening when Dahlia looks around the kitchen, where Eric, John, and Carlene have gathered with us for a Sunday night supper, and asks, "Are we a family?" A few days later, Carlene and I go out of town for a week to write. John puts Dahlia to bed when Justin has to work one night. Eric picks her up at school the next day, makes her mac and cheese, and gives her a bath. On the one hand, how we live is the answer, one that destroys the question. On the other hand, I think about what a singleton friend of mine, orphaned before her college graduation, says with longing: "I've always wanted a blood-related fact-checker." Is that what family is? If it is, then Dahlia has a family of three. Is it the emergency contacts in your kid's file at school? If that's the answer, then her family starts to grow. Is the question a personal one, or a societal one? Dahlia knows what *feels* like family. I wonder if that's enough.

There's a reason this book is not a memoir. Other people may define me as an only child, often relying on the elements of the stereotype I embody. But it's not the narrative I have chosen for myself, despite my drive to write a book about it. I am someone who has found both liberation and powerlessness in being an only child. I can imagine even if I hadn't been outnumbered by my parents I would have found a similar balance between the oppression and freedom of being their child. I'll never know how it would have been another way. I'll never know how growing up with bunk beds, instead of a lone twin, would have shaped me.

Last year we moved my childhood bed into Dahlia's room. When Justin and I were first dating and he would stay at my parents' house, his feet would stick out from between the spindles of its footboard. I would press my body to his, grateful that in such a slim space there was nowhere to go but closer together. Now, on most nights, I crawl into this bed to put Dahlia to sleep. I read her a story, and then Justin appears with a cup of milk to accompany her second book. Sometimes he lingers to read the last one, all tangled together in our twin bed family hug. Dahlia closes her sleepy eyes, smiling; the three of us, a single embrace.

NOTES

Throughout this book, I cited specific sources for data, so you would know in context where I was getting my information. That said, I wanted to offer a sketch of some important works I consulted, a brief tour through my binders and bookshelves.

No one has done more to assemble and analyze research on only children than Toni Falbo. The meta-analyses she conducted with Denise Polit provide excellent literature reviews and data from hundreds of studies; here is the classic: "Quantitative Review of the Only Child Literature: Research Evidence and Theory Development," *Psychological Bulletin* (1986). Of the same vintage— only-child research fell off after the mideighties—the eight papers she wrote or edited for *The Single-Child Family* (New York: The Guilford Press, 1984) remain relevant and informative. Collected in that book and otherwise, Polit's work on older onlies, and their family dynamics, also dates from a past era, but remains some of the most interesting material I've found, especially Denise F. Polit, Ronald L. Nuttall, and Ena V. Nuttall, "The Only Child Grows Up: A Look at Some Characteristics of Adult Only Children," *Family Relations* (1980). Falbo and Polit have been soundly up-dated by Steven Mellor in his paper, "How Do Only Children Differ from Other Children?" *The Journal of Genetic Psychology* (1990). On achievement, Judith Blake's work remains the stan-dard bearer, and her book *Family Size and Achievement* (Berkeley: University of California Press, 1992) offers a sizeable introduction to her data. Several other papers explore issues of stereotyping, no-tably Ann Laybourn, "Only Children in Britain: Popular Stereo-type and Research Evidence," *Children & Society* (1990) and, most recently, Adriean Mancillas, "Challenging the Stereotypes About Only Children: A Review of the Literature and Implications for Practice," *Journal of Counseling & Development* (Summer 2006); both offer terrific literature reviews. I found Carl Pickhardt's wis-dom to be indispensable in considering the realities of life as a singleton, both as a child and adult: *The Future of Your Only Child* (New York: Palgrave MacMillan, 2008).

While there may be a relative dearth of research on only chil-dren over the past few decades, there's been no shortage of liter-ature on well-being, policy, and economics related to the family. I find Nancy Folbre's economic analyses second to none, and this book in particular: *Valuing Children: Rethinking the Economics of the Family* (Cambridge, Mass.: Harvard University Press, 2010). Ann Crittenden's bestseller *The Price of Motherhood: Why the Most Important Job in the World Is Still the Least Valued* (New York: Pic-ador, 2010) is accessible and indispensable. The unhappiness of American parents is expertly dissected in Robin W. Simon's paper, "The Joys of Parenthood, Reconsidered," *Contexts* (Spring 2008), and this paper provides an excellent overview of a far wider map: Rachel Margolis and Mikko Myrskylä, "A Global Perspective on Happiness and Fertility," *Population and Development Review* (2011). I'm an admirer of Gerda Neyer's research and writing and find this paper to be a quite useful one: "Family Policies and Fertility in Europe," Max Planck Working Paper (2006). Ron Lesthaeghe's writing on the Second Demographic Transition has had a great influence on my thinking: "The Unfolding Story of the Second Demographic Transition," *Population and Development Review* (2010). And you can't get a better one-size-fits-all treatise on global warming and the ethics of family size—with a special focus on the choice to have an only child—than Bill McKibben's book *Maybe One: A Case for Smaller Families* (New York: Simon & Schuster, 1998).

As in all long-ranging book projects, only a fraction of the works I consulted found their way into the final distillation, not to mention the scores of interviews of both academics and only children that yielded my perspective beyond individual quotes and numbers. I am thankful to everyone who shared their stories, research, wisdom, and time.

ACKNOWLEDGMENTS

This book would not exist without the profound support of the following people: James and Judith Sandler; Eric Hynes (who for two years cared for this book like his own), Carlene Bauer and John Williams (IFLYG); Marin Sardy; Priscilla Painton, Michael Szczerban, Sydney Tanigawa, and Jonathan Karp; Elyse Cheney; the members of the Invisible Institute; Reva Jarvis, Averi Giudicessi, and Lacie Zassman; Molly Peterson, James and Lucas Nguyen; Jon and Terry Lane; and most of all, Justin and Dahlia Lane, my heart and my home.

ABOUT THE AUTHOR

auren Sandler has written on cultural politics and women's issues for publications including *Time, New York, Slate,* and *The New York Times* and is the author of a previous book, *Righteous.* You can find her at www.laurensandler.com.